THE DEPRESSION MIRACLE

*Seven Keys to Shattering the Chains of
Anxiety, Depression, and the Unfulfilled Life*

Published by Best Seller Publishing®, Pasadena, CA
Best Seller Publishing® is a registered trademark
Printed in the United States of America.

This publication is designed to provide accurate and authoritative information with regard to the subject matter covered. It is sold with the understanding that the publisher is not engaged in rendering legal, accounting, or other professional advice. If legal advice or other expert assistance is required, the services of a competent professional should be sought. The opinions expressed by the authors in this book are not endorsed by Best Seller Publishing® and are the sole responsibility of the author rendering the opinion.

Most Best Seller Publishing® titles are available at special quantity discounts for bulk purchases for sales promotions, premiums, fundraising, and educational use. Special versions or book excerpts can also be created to fit specific needs.

For more information, please write:

Best Seller Publishing®
1346 Walnut Street, #205
Pasadena, CA 91106
or call 1(626) 765 9750
Toll Free: 1(844) 850-3500
Visit us online at: www.BestSellerPublishing.org

Table of Contents

Introduction

Do you find yourself living the nightmare of mental illness? Do you need help shattering the chains of anxiety and depression that are holding you hostage in your mind? Is your life unfulfilled, and do you feel stuck in the rut of unsatisfied dreams?

If your answer to any of these questions is yes, then let me ask you this very important question: *How long do you want to stay exactly the way you are right now?* Do you want to stay this way for a month? A year? Five years? Another 10 years? Or, sadly, do you want to stay this way for the rest of your life? Please take a minute and think about what I just asked you.

I hope your answer is that you don't want to stay where you are with the challenges of mental illness or an unfulfilled life for one more day.

In this book, you will learn how to discover an inner strength you never knew you had. You will learn to see life as a classroom in which the challenges we are given from God and the Universe are to help us learn and grow. They are not punishments from an angry God or an angry Universe, and you were not chosen out of all the people in the world to have a terrible, frightening, or unfulfilled life.

You will also discover ways to remove fear from your life. Fear is one of the main evils that hold you back from making changes in you life. You will learn the important concept of knowing, trusting, and loving the real you – your inner self, your inner being. You will also be taught the primary way to lighten the burdens in your life.

Most importantly, you will be taught Seven Essential Keys to shatter the chains that hold you bound in your life.

Finally, you will be taught how to receive a miracle in your life by implementing and using these Seven Essential Keys. This miracle will bring peace, happiness, and freedom from the life that you now live.

Many people have asked me why I wrote this book. For 40 years, I lived in the darkest hell on earth. It was the hell of bipolar disorder, anxiety, severe paranoia, panic attacks, stress, terribly low self-esteem, and an unfulfilled life. With the Seven Essential Keys, a handpicked support group, medical help, and a miracle, I now live a life of happiness, peace, trust, and love. Most importantly, I now know who I am. My life has become fulfilled. I have found the real me and my purpose in life.

During my struggle with mental illness, the books, articles, and videos that made the most impact in my life were not written by doctors, psychiatrists, psychologists, or therapists. They were written by someone dealing with the same struggles as I had. They were written by patients and sufferers. For that reason, I felt an immediate connection to these people. I instantly trusted them and felt their pain. They understood what I was going through because they were enduring the same challenges. They didn't just learn about it from books, seminar, or tapes. Just like them, I am not a doctor, therapist, psychiatrist, or psychologist. I am a patient; I have lived it. I have lived the hell of these diseases and beaten them. With that said, I hope you and I can connect at the same level I did with them.

When I heard the following story, it made a huge impact on my life, and I knew I needed to write this book.

A guy was walking down the street, and he fell into a big hole. It was too deep for him to get out of it by himself. After a couple of hours, a priest walked by. The guy who had fallen into the hole asked, "Father, can you help me out of this big hole?" The priest said a prayer, and then he walked away. A few hours later, a doctor walked by. Again, the guy in the hole asked, "Hey Doc, can you help me out of this hole?" The doctor wrote a prescription and threw it in the hole. After several hours, when our guy was just about ready to give up, his best friend, Joe, walked by.

He shouted out, "Joe, can you help me out of this hole?" Joe replied, "Sure." Then he jumped down into the hole with him. Our guy said with a shocked look on his face, "Joe, are you stupid? Now we're both down in the hole." Joe looked at our guy and answered, "Yeah, but I have been down here before, and I know the way out."

I spent 40 years in the hole. Through the Seven Essential Keys and the teachings that I share with you in this book, I found a way out of the hole. Now I want to show you along with thousands of others the way out of the hole. You will be taught by someone who has been there, done that, and beat it. That is what is most important about this book. I discovered the keys along my journey of 40 years in the hole. I have experienced a miracle in my life along with using these keys, and I have beaten my depression, anxiety, panic, and mental illness. I know that if you use these keys daily, you will not have to wait and fight for as long as I had to.

In each chapter, you will find a detailed instruction of how to implement each of the Seven Essentials Keys we discuss. Each chapter is filled with important and helpful quotes, and especially inspiring stories from my life and the lives of others who have gone through the same experiences as you.

The greatest help I got in my journey was listening to people who knew what it was like to go through it. If today is the day you want to start changing your life, now is the time to start, and this book is the key.

Foreword

By Kimberly Giles

I have been greatly inspired by the writing of Viktor Frankl, a psychotherapist who survived horrendous circumstances in the Nazi concentration camps during World War II. He wrote a book called *Man's Search for Meaning*, which the Library of Congress named one of the ten most influential books ever written. He discovered that despite his terrible circumstances he had the power to choose his attitude about his circumstances, no matter how difficult they were.

I didn't believe I had the power to think positively in a horrible situation, at least not at first. It was difficult for me to accept. During periods of intense suffering, I couldn't get control of my thinking and I didn't see how finding meaning in my suffering would change how horrible it was. People told me to think positive, but these were people who weren't suffering themselves and had no idea what I was going through.

Greg Thredgold, like Viktor Frankl, has been through extremely rough experiences in his journey. He didn't share some his most painful life experiences in this book, but I want you to know…Greg knows about struggle and suffering. No matter what you are going through, Greg Thredgold understands it. He knows how you feel and how bad it can get. No matter how painful your current situation is, or how alone you feel, Greg has been there. For these reasons, he also knows the way through. Greg has risen above some horrendous trials in his life and refused to let depression, rejection, abuse, grief or misery beat him. He is an inspiration and a wise guide to follow.

He has decided to use what suffering has taught him, along with the Seven Essential Keys to make a difference in the world, and more importantly to help YOU feel better about YOUR situation. He prays daily that YOU will find peace, encouragement and determination from his story and the lessons he has learned along the way. If you will take the time to not just read this book, but stop, and do the exercises and things he recommends, it will pay off. You will find your load lightened to some extent and your hope and optimism will grow.

When you are faced with really terrible and difficult circumstances in life, one of two things usually happens. You will either let your struggles beat you, which might mean giving up or accepting a life of victimhood - or you (like Greg) will use your struggles to become wiser and stronger. You will use them to help you lift and serve others.

I believe God and the Universe want you to experience joy, happiness and beauty in this life. Our real purpose for being on the planet is to learn, and maybe more specifically to learn to love ourselves, and other people. I believe it is in getting outside of our own pain and lifting those around us that we experience the greatest joy there is, the joy of knowing we made a difference.

The American writer Leo Rosten said, "The purpose of life is not to be happy - but to matter, to be productive, to be useful, to have it make some difference that you have lived at all."

Greg is going to give you lots of amazing advice in this book to help you handle and rise above your challenges, but I hope you will be most inspired by his example. If he can turn his trials and struggles into a passion for serving others, and instead of complaining about his lot, focus his energy on helping others – you can too. The Seven Essential Keys and your miracle are waiting.

You can do this.

Chapter 1

The Strongest Among Us

As you learned from the Introduction, you and I have a lot of common ground. We have been crippled by some of the same things. We have realized that life is hard and does not always go the way we want it to go.

For us, life does not seem fair. It feels like God or the Universe is picking on us and that He or it might be upset or mad at us. I am here to tell you that that is not the truth. I have learned that God and the Universe give the gift of struggles to his strongest children – to the strongest among us.

Mark Twain said: "The two most important days in your life are the day you are born and the day you find out why."[1] In the Introduction, I asked you: How long do you want to stay the way that you are right now? If you are not fulfilling your destiny right now, you are probably miserable. Now, what are the consequences of being miserable all the time? Be completely honest with yourself. What does being miserable cost you? What do you lose if you are unhappy? On the flip side, what would be different in your life if you had a more positive attitude? What would you get if you were more optimistic? What would happen if you started to see yourself reaching your goals and dreams?

Those are important questions that everybody needs to ask themselves. Take time now to write down these questions and answer them.

---

[1] A Quote by Mark Twain. (n.d.). Retrieved September 22, 2015, from http://www.goodreads.com/quotes/505050-the-two-most-important-days-in-your-life-are-the

There were several times in my life when I wanted to change and get better, but then fear immediately jumped in. It prevented me from having the life I always wanted to have. I would get so caught up in my fears and be so overwhelmed that I would get to the point of saying that it is just not worth it. It is not worth the work. It is not worth the energy. It's not worth failing again. It is probably not going to work anyway. By the time I was ready to start something, I was drained of energy just by the thought of getting started. My energy, my motivation, my positive attitude, and my drive were all gone.

Over the past 40 years, I have had my share of miserable days. Some of those days I did not know if I was going to make it through or not. Some days I had to get through by trying to survive 5 or 10 minutes at a time. I would tell myself that I could make it another 5 or 10 minutes.

The amazing thing is that my track record for getting through those impossible days is 100%. I got through every single one of them; I have a perfect record.

If you are reading this book, your track record for getting through impossible days is 100% as well. That tells me that you are very strong. You are much stronger than you think you are. God, the Universe, or Higher Power, or whatever you believe in is not going to give you more than you can handle. Take a few minutes and think about your success rate.

Depression, anxiety, paranoia, low self-esteem, and not feeling fulfilled are private matters. The strongest of us are the ones who cry behind closed doors. We fight the battles that nobody knows about. Others do not understand what we are going through. If you had a broken arm, everybody would run over to sign your cast. But when it is your brain that needs fixing, people turn and go the other way.

When I began moving from darkness to light, I was happier than I had ever been in my life. However, it was not just roses and perfect days as soon as that process began. The challenges kept coming into my life.

The challenges came to make me better and stronger and to help me learn who I am and why I am here. In the same way, there is a purpose to your challenges. I know there is with all my heart.

After I had beaten my depression and paranoia, stopped having panic attacks, and found some clarity of mind, I thought life was amazing. I was truly happy for the first time in 40 years. But God and the Universe had more challenges in store for me to make me even stronger.

I was in that happy state that I had searched for my whole life for about six weeks until August 22, 2014. At midnight that night, when my wife and I were in bed, we suddenly heard somebody banging forcefully on our door and ringing the doorbell.

We all know that phone calls in the middle of the night are usually not good news; neither is people banging on your door at midnight. Trust me!

The people at our door rang the doorbell and banged harder and harder. I went to the front door and opened it. It was two of the leaders of my local church. Their faces were white as sheets, and I was scared to death. I invited them in.

Instantly, my son Connor came to my mind. He was in Taipei, Taiwan, on a two-year volunteer mission for our church. He had been in Taiwan for 15 weeks.

The church leaders came in and sat down. Then they proceeded to tell us that my son and his companion had been found dead in their apartment in Sanchong, Taiwan.

They did not know what had happened or how they had died. All they could tell us was that they had not been harmed or murdered. They thought that it might have been carbon monoxide poisoning. Months later, we found out that it was the cause of their deaths.

I thought that the journey through depression, paranoia, anxiety, and panic attacks was the worst hell you could ever experience. But when I lost Connor, who was 19 years old, I learned that there was a pain that was even worse. I did not know that something could hurt so much though I have heard it said that the hardest thing you could ever do in life is bury your child. It is true.

Years prior, I had made a decision that I was going to get better from my depression. I had put myself in a place where I was able to handle what was to come, good or bad. If I had been in a depressed state and full of fear when my son died, I don't know if I would have made it through that day. Two members of our family might have died that day.

I have learned that God or the Universe doesn't stop bad things from happening to us. God's job is to heal us from the pain that the bad things inflict on us, and to make us better and stronger.

For every wound we have, there is a scar, and every scar tells a story. People like you and me have so many scars, but the story that our scars tell is that we have survived because we are the strongest that God and the Universe have. We have survived 100% of the days that we have had to deal with our crushing challenges. I want to help you through the Seven Essential Keys to turn your wounds into wisdom.

Life is a classroom, and we have all been given different classes in the school of life. Some classes or challenges are physical. Some are mental. Some are spiritual. Some are dealing with relationships. And some are financial. Whatever they are in your life, they are all classrooms that you have been given. Take a few minutes and think about the concept of your life as a classroom.

I was given a mental health challenges classroom early on in my life. There is a reason I was given that class, and I needed to learn why it was given to me. I have learned that is not a punishment. God or the Universe is not mad at me. It is a classroom. It is a challenge that will allow me to learn and grow.

It took me 40 years of learning and dealing with the challenges till I found my life's purpose of being a life coach. Everything I have learned in my many years of struggle was to prepare me to help others. I have focused all my energy to help others who battle with the same issues. That is my "why" that Mark Twain's quote talked about earlier in this chapter. I feel like I have earned a PhD in depression, anxiety, paranoia, and the unfulfilled life because I have dealt with it for 40 years. I understand it!

Lessons Learned in My Classrooms

The biggest obstacle that I had to overcome was myself. It was not the depression. It was not the anxiety. It was not the paranoia. It was not the low self-esteem. It was not that I was unfulfilled. The biggest obstacle was me. I had to change myself. No one else was going to do it. It was my job.

I also learned that both you and I are where we are in life right now because of the decisions that we have made. I needed to stop blaming other people. Boy, did I have a long list of people to blame for ending up the way I did. But it was my decisions that got me to where I was. And it was my decisions that were going to make me either better or worse. It was my decisions that would keep me right where I was. I had to decide how long I wanted to stay where I was. Again, no one else was going to do it for me.

I learned the hard lesson that I am the sole owner of my thoughts and emotions. That is tough when you are depressed because you do not always think clearly. It is imperative that you learn and accept this lesson in order to start the change process in your life. I learned to ask God and the Universe to help me think straight and be at peace. At times, I was given that tender mercy of peace for the amount of time I needed to make a decision. I was in charge of what happened in my life.

Another fact I came to terms with was that the past is gone, and I cannot get it back, change it, or make it go away. What I could do was learn to see the past with clarity. I learned that I needed to stop living in the past. If you were to learn about my past, you would say, "Why would you want to go back there?" It was quite appalling. The past is gone. I cannot change those experiences or relive that time in my life. Instead, I need to be in the present, and I need to focus on what I want to happen in the future. We can't be moving forward if we are always looking back. How much time do you spend looking back?

Whether you like it or not, here is the greatest trick of all about life that I learned: We are not given a good life or a bad life. It is not like we come to earth, and some people get a good life while others get a bad one. We are given our life, period. It is up to us and only us to make it good or bad. The classroom that you are in right now is not a punishment. You are there make you a stronger and better person and to love and to give.

I also learned that no one person or thing is going to fix your life for you. People and things can aid in the changes that you will make. However, no doctor, no therapist, no counselor, no hospital, no religious leader, no book, no talk, no medication, and no friend or family member is going to do it for you. They can only help and be supportive. All of the above are important, but they are not going to do it for you. In the same way, this book is not is the cure. It is an aid. It is a motivation to help you use the Seven Essential Keys to getting better. You have to use them. You cannot just read about them. I give you tough love in this book. I give you straight talk. I say these things because I want you to get better and become the person you were meant to be.

It is up to you to embrace your life's challenges and fight like you have never fought before. That is how you will regain control of your life and find your miracle like I found mine. It's your choice.

The best quote I have ever heard on the topic of reality is by Alex Haley, the author of the book *Roots*. Mr. Haley said: "Either you deal what is the reality, or you can be sure that the reality is going to deal with you."[2] I learned the hard way that reality is going to deal with you.

I spent many years of my sickness getting ready to get ready, to get better. I thought that when I found the perfect therapist, I would get better. When I took the perfect medication, I would get better. When I had the

---

[2] Alex Haley Quotes. (n.d.). Retrieved September 22, 2015, from http://thinkexist. com/quotation/either_you_deal_with_what_is_the_reality-or_you/189174.html

perfect psychiatrist, I would get better. When I read the perfect book, I would get better. But until one of those things would happen, I was going to keep getting ready to get ready. This is a major reason it took 40 years.

I was living in the world of "someday I will do it." Another life lesson is "Someday is not a day of the week." Someday never comes. Someday is not on the calendar. Today is on the calendar. My life changed when I realized that it is a classroom and that I needed to trust the process of life. That was easier said than done for someone in the midst of the emotional and mental challenges that I have described. Take a few minutes and tell yourself that the word someday is being replaced with today in your life.

You and I have been placed in certain classrooms for a purpose. No matter what misfortune befalls you, you can be sure there are meaning and purpose to it. You are not suffering for nothing, and you will not do so. You will gain wisdom and strength from every experience. You are here to learn how to grow, trust, and love, and to find your purpose.

As a life coach, I have learned that most people already know the answers to their problems. They just don't trust themselves, and they don't trust life. They are consumed with paralyzing fear. I know this because I was for decades. We will talk about fear in depth in a future chapter.

I am sorry that God and the Universe gave us this class. It is a hard class for each of us. But I believe that someday, you will be proud of yourself for surviving it and becoming a better and stronger person in the process. I know it is a difficult concept to accept, but this new mindset and perspective and the Seven Essential Keys saved my life. It gave me my life back, and I want nothing more than for that to happen to you.

One day in my late 20s, I was with my wife and children at a shopping mall. While we were there, I wandered off to the end of an avenue, an empty lot, because I had a severe attack of paranoia, anxiety, and panic.

When my wife found me, I had a broken bottle, and I was ready to slit my wrists. Two hours later, I was checked into a psychiatric unit at a hospital in Phoenix. I didn't have much choice whether I was going or not.

When I was taken to the psychiatric unit, they took me through a big blue door. What I was told behind that door was that the job of the doctors and the nurses there was not to make me better. It was to make me stable on medication and then kick me back into the real world.

In that psychiatric unit, there were people who had decided that this was what they wanted for their lives. They could stay in that unit for so many days before the government would not pay any more, and they would have to leave. Then, a couple of weeks later, they could come back for another 45 days or so. This was their life.

There I made a friend whose name is Bob. He had played the game – come and gone to the psychiatric unit – for 30 years. It was all he wanted in life. He was an amazing man. We became very close even though we had nothing in common except our diseases.

I did not want to play the game that Bob played. Many like him were where they wanted to be. They had made up their minds. But I decided that my life was worth fighting for and that whatever would happen, I was going to get better. Whatever I was asked to do or try, I would do 150%. I was going to beat this disease, and I did not care how long it would take. I decided that my life was worth fighting for.

Today is the perfect day for you to acknowledge and shout out loud, "My life is worth fighting for. Do it now!

Chapter 2
The Achievers

I love doing what people tell me I can't do with my life. Accomplishing things that others said I couldn't do has given me a lot of joy. Especially when you have lived a life of depression, anxiety, panic, stress, and an unfulfilled satisfaction with what you have accomplished, many might have told you not even to try because they don't want to see you fail. They might say, "You are depressed. You are not going to be able to accomplish anything, so just accept that." They just want to love and protect you, but it's a negative love. It says you can't accomplish anything.

One of the things that helped me on my journey to overcoming my illness was discovering other people who suffered from the same things as I did and the amazing things that they had accomplished in their lives. I have compiled a list of just such people. It's an impressive list of people who have dealt with the same things that you and I deal with every single day.

- Abraham Lincoln (president) dealt with depression.
- David Bowie (musician) had very low self-esteem.
- Barbara Bush (former first lady) suffered from depression.
- Ludwig van Beethoven (composer) was bipolar.
- Ellen DeGeneres (comedian) suffers from depression.
- Mariah Carey (singer) has a very low self-esteem.
- Michelangelo (artistic genius) suffered from depression.

- Barbara Streisand (actress and singer) has a social phobia and anxiety.
- Serena Williams (tennis player) has very low self-esteem.
- Charles Dickens (author) suffered from depression.
- Donny Osmond (entertainer) has a panic disorder.
- Thomas Edison (inventor) suffered from depression.
- Kate Winslet (Academy Award-winning actress) has suffered from low self-esteem.
- Sir Anthony Hopkins (actor) has suffered from depression.
- Winston Churchill (English prime minister) was bipolar.
- Harrison Ford (actor) has suffered from depression.
- Ernest Hemingway (author) was bipolar and had an anxiety disorder.
- Mark Twain (author, humorist) was bipolar.
- Jim Carrey (actor) has suffered from depression.
- George Washington (president) suffered from depression.
- Oprah Winfrey (talk show host) suffers from anxiety.
- Will Smith (actor) suffers from low self-esteem.[3]

When I read that list, I realized that I am in great company. Hopefully, you realized the same thing. Some of the people with the greatest achievements in the world have suffered from what you and I suffer from. But let me strongly clarify: They did not achieve their greatness because they had these illnesses. They achieved their greatness *in spite of* these illnesses. We are not what happen to us. We are what we choose to become. It is our choice to become what we want to become in

---

[3] *Famous People with Biological Brain Disorders.* (n.d.). Retrieved September 22, 2015, from http://www.bark4care.org/B4C/Resources.html

life whether we have these challenges or not. Like these great men and women, we can achieve great things in spite of our challenges.

Steps to Change

To change and achieve greatness in your life, you have to be enthusiastic. That doesn't mean you ignore the hard-hitting aspects of your life and the terrible days that you experience. Nevertheless, we need to be enthusiastic. Enthusiasm brings on change. It is a very hard thing for a depressed person to have, I know. I had that challenge. What you need to do is center on being positive as much as you can until it becomes a habit. You need to have a desire to change enough to be positive most of the time.

Through the journey of implementing these changes, you need to find out what works for you. Not everything I have tried is going to work for you. Not everything you have tried would work for me. Take a minute and think about what has and has not worked for you.

Don't be discouraged by early disappointments. Time after time, I would get ready to make a change, and I would think that I was going to beat my illnesses. Then, when the first thing I tried wouldn't work, I would think I failed, so I would quit. Don't let this happen to you.

Failure is an immense part of success. Every person in the list above failed many, many, many times before they became successful. You have to find out what works for you and what keeps you positive most of the time. You can surround yourself with a support group. Hopefully, you have done so even before today. Find support from others. I found support from these famous people. There are support groups, books, tapes, blogs, medical professionals, and dear friends that you can trust that will be there for you no matter what. Put together that support group. It will help you get better, and it will help you through the tough days. You don't have to do this by yourself.

Ralph Waldo Emerson said: "What lies behind us and what lies before us are tiny matters compared to what lies within us."[4] I want to help you peel away the layers of anxiety, panic, low self-esteem, and depression. As we peel away those layers, we will find the real you, the person that God or the Universe created and sent to this earth to accomplish great things.

We need to be very careful of those around us that support us. I have had many therapists over 40 years. One of them hurt me so badly with what he said that it set back my recovery about five years. Perhaps he said what he said out of love. I don't know. But it was wrong!

In my first session with him, he said: "I have a test that I want you to take. This is a test that was given to 10,000 inmates in prison – the worst 10,000 inmates we could find. They were rapists, murderers, and the most violent vicious men they could find. We had them take the test to establish where their level of self-esteem was. I want you to take the test so that we can see where your self-esteem is compared to theirs."

I went home and took the test, which consisted of several hundred extremely personal questions. I answered them all honestly, and it took four hours. After I had completed the test, I took it back to the therapist with great anticipation.

A couple of sessions later, he had my test results. I was quite intrigued to know where I stood. He showed me a line on a graph and said:

"This is the average of the murderers, rapist, and killers – the worst people we could find on the earth. This is where their self-esteem is."

"Well, where is my self-esteem?" I asked.

"Greg, your self-esteem didn't even show up on this chart," he answered. Then he continued: "You have the lowest self-esteem I have ever seen in any person I have ever met in my entire life."

---

4   A Quote by Ralph Waldo Emerson. (n.d.). Retrieved September 22, 2015, from http://www.goodreads.com/quotes/15579-what-lies-behind-us-and-what-lies-before-us-are

That was a crushing blow to me. My self-esteem was practically nonexistent. Early in my life, I was told that when you have that kind of negative event happen, you can get angry, or you can get excited. Both of those emotions create action.

At that point, I felt that I had two options. I could go home and just shrivel up in a corner and wish I was dead, or I could get angry. Well, I got angry. I got angry with the therapist because he was wrong. Then I made the decision to quit going to that therapist. I continued to study people who had been told they couldn't do something, and a new list started to come to together for me.

- Michael Jordan was told that he was no good at basketball, and he was cut from his high school basketball team. At first, he went home and cried. Then he got angry.
- The Beatles were told by a record executive that they had no future in show business.
- Walt Disney was told he had no imagination or original ideas, and they fired him from a job.
- Oprah Winfrey was fired from a job and told she was not fit for television.
- Albert Einstein didn't speak till he was almost four years old. He was told he would never amount to anything in his life.[5]
- I, Greg Thredgold, was told that I have the lowest self-esteem this therapist had ever seen in any person. I made the choice to change. I got angry.

Some of these people got angry, and some got excited. They made a decision to change. They failed many times in the process of becoming

---

5   Stovall, J. (2013, March 12). *Failure Isn't Final*. Retrieved September 22, 2015, from http://www.refreshleadership.com/index.php/2013/03/failure-isnt-final/

successful. You can't leave footprints in the sands of time if you're sitting on your butt. Who of you wants to leave buttprints in the sands of time?

If There Were No Risk of Failure

What would you attempt to do if you knew you could not fail? The first time I was asked that question, fear jumped into my mind, and I thought: "That's a terrible question. Even if I couldn't fail, I would still fail. I wouldn't try anything that hard. What if I did fail?" Many of you probably had the same reaction as I did.

Fear, more than any other emotion, keeps people from achieving their goals. The crazy thing about fear is it's not real. It's just a thought, a feeling. However, if we feed it and give it attention, it's a very powerful thought. Fear can paralyze and destroy us.

Kimberly Giles is my life coach. I have the blessing of working as a life coach in her company, Clarity Point Coaching. In her book, *Choosing Clarity: The Path to Fearlessness*, she wrote:

> Every day is a grand adventure into the great unknown and you cannot know what lies around the next corner. So, standing in this place, with the unknown before you, you have only two choices: you can live in trust (believing you are safe and that good things are coming) or you can live in fear (scared of the future and focused on you). Your choice will not change what's around that next corner, it will be what it's meant to be, but it will have a big impact on the way you feel today. Do you want to experience today in fear, focused on yourself? Or do you want to experience trust and focus on love? It's up to you.[6]

Again, my question is: What would you attempt to do in your life if you could not fail? One of the things I had to discover when I truly and honestly tried to answer that question was that during my whole

---

[6] Quotes About Life Adventure. (n.d.). Retrieved October 5, 2015, from http://www.goodreads.com/quotes/tag/life-adventure

life, my family, friends, therapists, and other people who loved me had been telling me not to have big dreams. They said that I wasn't going to accomplish much because of my depression. They were constructing the plans for how I should live my life. I couldn't let that happen, and either can you!

One ad for Harley-Davidson motorcycles said: "When you write the story of your life, don't let anyone else hold the pen."[7] It's your life. You hold the pen and write it. It's nobody's job to write your life but you. I challenge you, even in your fear, to start by doing the following exercise.

Stop reading and do it now!

Take a blank page of paper and write about your positive future. Write about your goals and dreams. Write about living life and accomplishing whatever you want to accomplish. Let the words just flow onto the paper. It does not have to be perfect.

Writing it down gives you better ideas than just thinking about it. When we have goals, we need to write them down because a goal not written is only a wish.

Right now you have two options. You can do the exercise, or you can ignore it. Well, we all know that if you don't move forward, you are moving backward. You can't move side-to-side in life, and there is no staying where you are. Doing nothing to move forward and getting farther away from the things you want to accomplish in your life is also a choice – your choice.

If you were to try to move forward, you would find something greater than what you have now. You would have to give up some fear and take control of your life, and you would accomplish something great in return.

---

[7]   Chahal, G. (2014, March 17). "When You Write the Story of Your Life, Don't Let Anyone Else Hold the Pen" [Web log post]. Retrieved October 5, 2015, from http://www.huffingtonpost.com/gurbaksh-chahal/when-you-write-the-story-_b_4951003.html

Perhaps you're thinking, "But Greg, what if I fail?" As a famous quote says, "What if you fly?" What if you accomplish something? What an amazing thing that will be for you! I know. I am experiencing it because I made choices to try things that were scary and difficult. Our family has developed the motto "We can do hard things."

In reality, life doesn't come with absolute guarantees like you are not going to fail. The fear of failure keeps most people from moving ahead in their life whether it's mentally, spiritually, physically, or emotionally. Bill Walsh, NFL football coach, said: "Failure is part of success, an integral part."[8] The best way to gauge your progress in reaching a goal is to look at the number of setbacks and failures that you have had. If you have not yet failed in what you are attempting to do, chances are you are not trying hard enough. You are not wholeheartedly pursuing your goal. Fear is still holding you back. You must fight like you never have for these changes.

Thomas Edison is the best example of someone who kept trying after experiencing failure. How many times did he fail to find the right filament for his light bulb? It was 10,000 times. The way he said it was: "I have not failed. I've just found 10,000 ways that won't work."[9]

"Failure is simply the opportunity to begin again, this time more intelligently,"[10] said Henry Ford. Imagine if you only tried doing things once and never tried again if you failed. I'm quite certain that the first time you tried to walk you fell. What if you were to quit right then? You would be crawling still. Or how about the first time you tried to talk, and nobody understood you? Feeding yourself was probably not a great

---

[8] *Mad As Hell And... Quotes of the Day – Saturday, September 19, 2015 – Bill Walsh.* (2015, September 19). Retrieved September 22, 2015, from http://madashelland.com/?p=15245

[9] Thomas A. Edison Quote. (n.d.). Retrieved September 22, 2015, from http://www.brainyquote.com/quotes/quotes/t/thomasaed132683.html

[10] Henry Ford Quote. (n.d.). Retrieved September 22, 2015, from http://www.brainyquote.com/quotes/quotes/h/henryford121339.html

success the first time either. Or how about the first time you tried to get yourself dressed or the first time you used the bathroom? Jack Canfield, the author and speaker said: "Don't worry about failures, worry about the chances you miss when you don't even try."[11]

To close this chapter, I want to share one of my conversations with my coach, Kimberly Giles. One time I was in a session with her, we were discussing this very subject of what you could you do if you couldn't fail. I was going through the fear that I would fail. I didn't want to put anything down on paper because I was convinced I would fail since I had failed so many times before. I had a very bad attitude. I told Kim, "I don't want to do this."

I remember Kim closing her book, looking me straight in the eye, and saying: "Okay, Greg, you have a choice right now. It's your life. You have a choice. We can quit the coaching right now. We will say goodbye, and you can leave. You can tell everybody that you failed and decided

not to get any better. Or you can have some faith in what is being taught and continue to peel away the layers till we find the real you that I know is here to achieve greatness." It was that tough love I talked about in the last chapter. Luckily, I made the right decision to move on. I promise as you make an effort to improve, God and the Universe will bring people into your life to help. Kim was one of those people in my life.

Martin Luther King, Jr. said these amazing words: "Faith is taking the first step even when you don't see the whole staircase."[12]

---

[11] A Quote from Chicken Soup for the Soul. (n.d.). Retrieved September 22, 2015, from http://www.goodreads.com/quotes/29794-don-t-worry-about-failures-worry-about-the-chances-you-miss

[12] Martin Luther King, Jr. Quote. (n.d.). Retrieved September 22, 2015, from http://www.brainyquote.com/quotes/quotes/m/martinluth105087.html

Chapter 3
Key 1: Fear

"Everything you want is on the other side of fear."[13]
— Jack Canfield, author of *Chicken Soup for the Soul*

In this and the next few chapters, I will discuss the Seven Essential Keys that I have found throughout my journey. These keys were essential to my recovery and beating my mental illness. They might be basic things that everybody needs in their life, but they are even more important for someone dealing with depression, anxiety, and fear that is out of control. By using the Seven Keys daily, you are on the way to gaining freedom and shattering the chains that are holding you bound.

What It Means to Be Brave

We began discussing fear in the previous chapter, and in this chapter we will dig much deeper. Bravery is the opposite of fear. When I say bravery, what do you think of? Contrary to what you might think, the definition of bravery is different for everybody. It comes in different shapes and sizes depending on what we are being challenged with.

I have had days where getting out of bed was brave for me. Walking outside to get in my car was brave. Even trying to get through work took all the bravery I could come up with.

---

[13] Jack Canfield Quotes. (n.d.). Retrieved September 22, 2015, from https://www.goodreads.com/author/quotes/35476.Jack_Canfield

Many of the movies that have come out in the last few years have been about superheroes. Some have been about the superheroes that were around when we were kids, and others have been about newly invented ones. Real-life heroes don't have perfect lives free from fear. They are just so focused on their goals that they can't turn back. Their goals have simply become more important than the fear. Being brave requires you to feel fear. Every time you feel scared, overwhelmed, and full of fear, you should view that as an opportunity to be brave.

Dr. Henry Link said: "We generate fears while we sit. We overcome them by taking action. Fear is nature's way of warning us to get busy."[14] When we sit, we feed the fear, and it gets bigger and bigger. Even though it's just an emotion, it can appear so real that it can feel like chains wrapping themselves around us. I have had days when it has made me not even want to get out of bed. But we can't let the fear paralyze us. There is a Swedish proverb that says: "Worry often gives a small thing a big shadow."[15] What we worry about can be insignificant, but the worry and fear can make the shadow of it seem so huge that it takes over our whole life and dictates how we live. Take a few minutes and think about the fears in your life.

Bob Proctor is one of my favorite speakers and writers. He said: "Faith and fear have a lot in common, they both demand you believe in something you cannot see."[16] Through my life and studies, I have learned that fear is not real: it's just an emotion. Its power comes from

---

[14] Tailwind Blog. (2014, July 31) We generate fears while we sit. We overcome them by action. Fear is natures way of warning us to get busy. – Dr. Henry Link. [Web log post]. Retrieved September 22, 2015, from http://blog.tailwindapp.com/best-business-quotes/link/

[15] A quote by Swedish Proverb. (n.d.). Retrieved September 22, 2015, from http://www.goodreads.com/quotes/659751-worry-often-gives-a-small-thing-a-big-shadow

[16] Proctor, B. [bobproctorLIVE] (2013, March 14). Faith and fear have a lot in common, they both demand you believe in something you cannot see...[Tweet] Retrieved September 22, 2015, from https://twitter.com/bobproctorlive/status/312039970850365441

how we let it affect us. It comes from how we have been trained and how we have listened to different people in our life. Faith is something I can't see, but I know it's real because I have at times let it control my life. It's not something that I think is real. It is real, even though I can't see it.

You have to decide what goal can outshine your fear. As Les Brown, the amazing speaker, said: "Too many of us are not living our dreams because we are living our fears."[17] Your life can't be all about your doubts and fears. You need to have dreams and goals, which we discussed that in the last chapter. If you are living controlled by your fears, you have to start living your dreams a little bit at a time. That is all it takes to get started. Let your goals outweigh your fears.

At a certain point, we need to stop just thinking about it. We need to stop being scared of it; we need to stop getting ready to get ready. We need to stop procrastinating; we need to stop letting fear destroy our lives. We need to take action. These actions can be little things, and we need to recognize when we accomplish those things. We also need to recognize our failures because they are a part of our success.

I want to share some numbers with you. I'm going to touch on them briefly in this chapter, and I will expand on them at the end of the book. They are 45, 17, 4, and 1.

I tried 45 different medications on my journey to get better; that is more than one a year. I had some medications that did nothing. I had other medications that put me in a fog and made me feel as if I was on the outside of life looking in. They would take away all my emotions, both good and bad. I didn't feel depressed, but I didn't feel happy either; I was numb. Then I had one medication that I classify as medication from hell because it almost killed me.

The next number is 17. I had 17 different therapists, psychiatrists, and psychologists. Some I only went to once or twice. Others I visited

---

[17] Les Brown quote. (n.d.). Retrieved September 22, 2015, from http://www.brainyquote.com/quotes/quotes/l/lesbrown384269.html

weekly for years. Any of them would tell you I was a straight "A" student; I did everything they asked me to do. I did every exercise. I read every book. I took every test. I answered every question because I had made up my mind to get better.

The number four is the number of times I was in mental hospitals in the psychiatric unit, behind the big doors. I was there anywhere from a week to two weeks per visit. Usually, I was there on suicide watch, or I had just stopped taking my medication and didn't tell anybody until I suffered the dreadful consequences.

The last number is the number one. That is how many miracles I needed to get better. It took 40 years. I know by using these Seven Essential Keys, you miracle will come sooner. I will tell you about it in detail at the end of the book. It not only saved my life, but it also gave me life. I had to be unbelievably brave to try what I was told to try because everybody that knew about it told me not to, except for my family. I had to be extremely courageous to do all those things. But getting better was more important to me than staying where I was.

Mary Anne Radmacher, author and trainer, said: "Courage doesn't always roar. Sometimes courage is the quiet voice at the end of the day saying I'll try again tomorrow."[18] Hundreds of the days of my journey, that was my bravery. I was going to wake up the next day, and I would keep trying because that is all I could do. And I succeeded; my track record for getting through the tough days and being brave is 100%.

Taking Control of Your Fear

We know we need to be brave, and we know we need to set goals. We also know those goals have to be more important to us than anything else. This is you fighting for your life. Take a few minutes and think about bravery.

---

[18]   Mary Anne Radmacher Quotes. (n.d.). Retrieved September 22, 2015, from http://www.goodreads.com/author/quotes/149829.Mary_Anne_Radmacher

How do you take control of fear? There is a phobia called phobophobia, which is the fear of fear. It's the fear of being afraid. Boy, did I have that. I always found it interesting how the concept of playing it safe makes many people choose to be miserable over being happy. They would rather stay in a place where they are miserable than take one small step to try to be happy. They have been paralyzed by their fear. That is not how life has to be.

Fear only becomes real when we believe in our minds that it's real. It's created by our subconscious mind. It's nothing more than an emotion and a feeling. When we see it and focus on it, it becomes real to us, and it grows. Then we self-sabotage, and we won't even try to get better. We procrastinate, and we become excessively anxious.

I used to be extremely anxious. Some days I would have dozens of panic attacks, and I would be so filled with panic that I couldn't function. We self-sabotage if we fail to set goals that we follow through on. In the last chapter, I challenged you to write them down. If you didn't, I plead with you to go back and do that now! That is the first step.

We tend to beat ourselves up with our negative self-talk. Instead of having negative thoughts of "I can't do it," change those thoughts to something positive. Start small and strive to become more positive every day till you reach the point where you are thinking "What if I could do that?"

Some of us will only try to do something if we believe we can do it perfectly. It's called perfectionism. It's a willingness to try only those things that you know you will finish perfectly because if it's not perfect, you feel like you have failed. The truth is you can't do anything perfectly; there is no such thing as perfection. Everything we do is short of perfection.

I have read about the amazing Persian rugs that cost thousands of dollars that they intentionally put a flaw in each one. It's a reminder that you cannot make anything that is perfect. Things cannot be perfect, and neither can you.

Think of fear and love as energies. Fear is the energy that contracts; it makes us smaller. It makes us wrap ourselves up in those chains and paralyze ourselves so that we can't accomplish anything; we don't even try. Love and trust are the energy that expands our lives. It expands our power, our belief, our goals, and our dreams. Fear contracts; love expands. Stay positive, believe, and take those small steps. Decide right now to expand your life.

Kimberly Giles, life coach wrote,

When you choose to be a state of trust and love, you literally can't experience fear. The emotions can't exist at the same time, in the same place. I call it the state of trust and love 'clarity' because it is the only state where the fog of fear is out of the way, so you can see your life as it is. [19]

It is essential to understand that trust and love cannot be in the same place as fear at the same time. You are filled with one or the other, and there is an amazing difference.

I want you to take a piece of paper and write "I want _____" and then fill in the blank. Then write "But I am afraid of _____" and then fill in the blank. You now have written something you want, and the reason you are afraid to reach for it. I want this to happen, but I'm afraid this is going to happen. Simply look at those two statements and start to believe that you feel more strongly about what you want than what you are afraid of. The thing you are afraid of is most likely fear based and not real.

It is easier said than done, but I made up my mind that I was going to beat my illness even if it killed me. To be honest, there were days when it almost did. The fear got that great, but I won, and I beat it.

---

[19] Giles, K. (2013, November 4). *Are you addicted to fear?* Retrieved September 22, 2015, from http://www.ksl.com/?nid=1010&sid=27484466

Just take one step toward your goal, one small step. Then, like when you learn to walk, take another little step towards accomplishing it. Knowing that you are getting closer to it will keep you positive. Keep your eye on that goal.

Wherever your attention and your focus go, that is where your life goes. As we talked about earlier, if your life is not going forward with those little steps, you are going backward. Life does not stand still.

Celebrate each little thing you accomplish. There will be times when you fail, but you will try again, smarter and more experienced. Eventually, you will accomplish what you set out to do. You can do this!

The moments when you accomplish what you want are called light bulb moments. When I coach my clients, I always try to have them point out their light bulb moments from the past week. I ask them: "What happened in your life? What light bulb went on and said 'I changed, I did it, I accomplished this little thing?'" Many times when my clients tell me how their week was, they skip right over the light bulb moment, the major change that they have been working on. I have to point it out to them that they must not miss these moments. Don't miss the little things or the big things. Celebrate every light bulb moment! Take a minute and think about your light bulb moments.

Your current largest fear carries your greatest thrill in your life. You will experience it by being aware of your little light bulb moments and by failing and trying again. You can be brave. You are much stronger than you think you are. You are one of those achievers we talked about; you are one of those strong soldiers that God and the Universe give their toughest challenges to.

About 15 years ago, I was about as low as you could get. I was full of panic, and my medication wasn't working; nothing was working. We had made the decision to move from Arizona to Utah because my parents were in Utah, and I needed to be there to help take care of them. They were approaching their 80s and starting to need some help.

At that time, I had to do three of the hardest things we do in life. As I go through these three, you will nod in agreement if you have done any one of them. I had to do all three of them at the same time.

First, I had to move a family of six 700 miles with the prayer that my kids would find good friends, that they would have good schools, and that we would find a nice neighborhood. Second, I had to buy a house without my wife seeing it ahead of time. I had to find the one that my wife would have picked if she were there. That is something that can get you in a lot of hot water as a husband. Third, I had to start a new job.

Those are three of the most stressful things we do in life, and I had to do them all at the same time. I was a wreck mentally, but I didn't have a choice. I had to be brave for my family and my parents.

I got up to Utah on a Saturday morning and met the realtor. I had two days to find a house because my job started the following Monday. I looked at 27 homes in a day and a half. God has a sense of humor because the perfect house that my wife would have picked was the 27th house I looked at, so I bought that house.

Then I had to start my new job. I was going to run a large department in a company. I was brought in to clean up the mess the previous bosses had left in this department. That in itself was a very stressful situation.

Lastly, we were moving our family. I was in Utah for 30 days before my family came. In other words, I was without my support system, which was my wife, kids, and friends, for a month, but I did it. It seemed impossible, but I got brave. Trust won over fear.

The move, the house, and the job became more important than my fear, and I was more focused on that than I was on the fear. I had a lot of faith, and I had trust. Sometimes I stumbled and thought it would never work, but I went back to trust and love and faith, and the fear wasn't there anymore.

"Those who fear the darkness have no idea what the light can do."[20] I spent years in the darkness, thinking there was no light at the end of the tunnel. The last few years, I have beaten the darkness, and I have found happiness and clarity. Though I still have challenges, the light is amazing. It can change your life if you will just taking those first few small steps.

---

[20]   *Sad Quotes and Sayings.* (n.d.). Retrieved September 23, 2015, from http://www.bestsayingsquotes.com/quote/those-who-fear-the-darkness-have-no-idea-what-the-light-can-1772.html

Chapter 4

Key 2: Trusting Yourself

The second key is trusting yourself. All the Seven Essentials Keys are important, but if you don't trust yourself, the rest of the keys will be ineffective. Trusting yourself is the foundation for the changes you want to make and for finding joy, happiness, and fulfillment and achieving your goals.

Get to Know the Real You

Shakespeare said, "To thine own self be true."[21] That is what we will discuss in this chapter. You need to get to know, trust, and love the real you. You are the one who is going to make the difference in your life. We have talked about having a support system of doctors, therapists, psychiatrists, psychologists, books, medication, family, friends, and whatever you have. Those things are all great, and they are essential to getting better, but without you believing and acting like you are going to get better, none of those things will work.

Believing in yourself is the beginning of your journey to where you want to go in life. It starts very small. We already touched on celebrating your light bulb moments and having long-term goals. We also discussed taking small steps and having goals that can be as little as hourly or daily – however small they need to be for you to start making changes in your

---

[21] William Shakespeare Quote. (n.d.). Retrieved September 23, 2015, from http://www.brainyquote.com/quotes/quotes/w/williamsha106104.html

life. Remember, a goal not written is only a wish. Write down every goal, no matter how small. Take a minute and review your goals.

There are people who believe in you and want you to succeed and be better, which is wonderful to have. However, that is worthless if you do not make the journey. Others can't do it for you.

I have an outstanding support system around me. I have an incredible wife, Cindy, who I have been married to for almost 31 years. I also have four wonderful children. They all desperately wanted me to get better, and they wanted to see me change. In addition, I have the support of friends and a church family. I have built this support system myself, the same way you will build yours.

I have spent a lot of time believing I couldn't get better and that there was no hope for me. I believed that I was a failure in the lives of those around me. I felt like I was just taking up space, and I thought that they would be much better off without me. I was wrong! That was the fear talking.

Nobody knows the real you but you. I spent years trying to find the real me, peeling away the layers of fear and doubt. Whether or not you knew yourself before the depression, anxiety, panic, or unfulfilled life came upon you, you might have lost connection with who you are after experiencing those challenges.

Now you are trying to find the real you, your inner self, your soul, the person that God and the Universe want you to be. But you have self-doubt. I understand that because I was loaded with it. I told you about where my self-esteem was when I started my journey. Self-doubt grows like a weed in our minds and our lives. Self-doubt is not something that you can fight because if you fight it, it's just going to get worse. You need to learn to tame and control it. You will always have it, so it's going to be part of your life. But as your learning grows, it will become a less powerful part of your life.

The entertainer and author Donny Osmond said: "You have to believe in yourself, otherwise you can't do it. If you don't believe in yourself, how do expect anyone else to? Because ultimately, you're the one who has to do it."[22] Donny Osmond used to suffer from a severe social phobia. It would sometimes freeze him even up to the minute he had to go on stage and perform. He thought his performance had to be perfect, and if he didn't feel that he could perform flawlessly, he would cancel the show. He had to work through this mindset, and it took time. He made the decision to beat his problem.

There will be times on your journey when everything goes wrong, and it will fall apart when people in your support system don't believe in you. You are going to feel alone, empty, and hopeless. That is the exact moment you must believe in yourself. You have to go back to the fact that your track record for getting through terrible days is 100%. You are going to get through that day, and you are going to get through the next tough day.

Never let anybody break your spirit and soul, no matter how close to you they are. You have to stand on your own two feet, and you have to stand up for yourself as if nobody else is going to. Unfortunately, we all have people around us who will give anything to see us fail. You must never give them that satisfaction. Hold your head up high, smile, and stand your ground. This is your life. You are in control of it, and nobody else can control it unless you let them.

Eventually, I learned that no matter how scary and distorted life can be when you are depressed, and you have anxiety and panic, life is safe. For many years, I felt that life was unsafe and out to get me. I believed that the Universe, God, or that Higher Power was angry with me and dissatisfied with my performance. Nothing could be further from the

---

[22] Donny Osmond Quote. (n.d.). Retrieved September 23, 2015, from http://www.brainyquote.com/quotes/quotes/d/donnyosmon401685.html?src=t_believe_in_yourself

truth. The sooner you can grasp and believe this fact, the sooner your journey to healing begins. Life is not out to get you.

I signed up for whatever was supposed to happen in my life. I believe that God and the Universe had a purpose for my journey and that the things that happened in my life were supposed to happen. My purpose in life was to spend 40 years fighting and crying to get better and beat my depression, anxiety, and panic. My learning experience for all those decades allows me to help countless people beat the same kinds of challenges.

That was my education, my life, and my journey. God and the Universe give their toughest test to the strongest children. I understand that now. I understood it more as I started to progress and take the small steps to get better. I had years where I thought that life was going just to end for me and everything would destroy me.

But none of what I imagined and feared ever came true because it was fear based. Fear is not real; it's an emotion. The leap of faith that I ask you to take in small steps is not just pushing yourself into the darkness, but diving into the light that those around you can see.

Learning to Trust Yourself Equals Living Life

You start living life once you learn to trust yourself even a little bit. We were sent to this earth to learn, grow, and serve other people. Earlier, we looked at famous people and the things they have accomplished in spite of dealing with the same things that you and I deal with every day. Jaye Miller said,

> Believing in yourself is not just for you; it's for every person who has touched your life in a significant way and for every person your life will touch the same way five minutes from now, or five centuries from now.[23]

---

[23] *Inspirational Thoughts About Believing in Yourself.* (2013, February 1). Retrieved September 23, 2015, from http://www.verybestquotes.com/inspirational-thought-for-the-day-02032013-believing-in-yourself/inspirational-thoughts-about-believing-in-yourself/

We need to have long-term ambitions and long-term goals, but to get there we will take extremely small steps at first. That is all I'm asking you to do: take extremely small steps with long-term ambitions.

Don't let yourself be pushed through life by your problems. You need to be led by your dreams. Your dreams, not your problems, are what you need to focus on. You need to help create amazing things in your life by taking small steps and by focusing on your dreams in spite of your challenges and problems. It's not an easy thing. But you need to understand that I have done it, and now I have dreams and goals that are both scary and exciting, but I can see myself accomplishing them down the road.

When I decided to write a book, I felt I had over 10,000 reasons for why I couldn't do it. I had never written a book. I did not like writing in school. English was my worst subject in school. It would have been so easy to stop at that point. However, as I thought about it and started taking small steps, that dream came true because you are reading my book. What I had to do was stop living in my past. Instead, I had to make a commitment to look and move forward.

You, like I did, have to make the decision. That is the first step. Decide to live your life and don't let anybody say you can't do it and believe them. It's your life!

What can easily happen is that though you try to move forward, you still look backward. You can't do that. You must decide to move forward. Trust in yourself and the process of life. Also, trust that life is safe and that you have a 100% perfect track record of getting through the tough days.

Now that I have beaten my challenges and I'm happy and have goals, is my life without self-doubt? No, not at all. But I can honestly say that I believe in myself like I never have in my life. There are other people who don't believe in me, and that is okay. I believe in me, and that is what changed my life. I still have self-doubt, but I have learned to control it.

I have learned to replace it with goals, dreams, and small steps. Taking small steps and sometimes failing are the keys to your success.

It's okay to put yourself out there without knowing if you will finish everything you want to do. Even if there are some people who don't believe you can accomplish it, you believe you can do it. And if you fail, that is okay as well. Failure is part of success. It is part of the journey. All it means is that you will do it differently next time.

Be Careful Whom You Tell

When I started changing and telling others my plan to beat my depression, my biggest concern was toxic people. We need to be careful whom we share our dreams, visions, and desires to get better with. Many people will immediately shoot down your ideas before they even understand them. They might say something like: "You are irresponsible. You can never do that. Why would you even think you could do that? Stop thinking like that; you're crazy." That is what some people said to me. Don't let them steal your new energy just because they have lost theirs. When you encounter toxic people, run away.

Everybody has toxic people around. They can even be people who are very close to us. Eventually, you have to get to a point where you can look at them and say, "Watch me do it."

Lots of people told me: "You're never going to be able to write a book." "You have never written a book. You don't even know how to write a book." Now I can say, "Ha-ha, I have written a book." I replaced those who said I couldn't write a book with people who have written books and know how to do it – people who believed that I could do it as well.

Best selling author Karen Quinones said: "When someone tells me 'no,' it doesn't mean I can't do it, it simply means I can't do it with them."[24] What a great lesson!

---

[24] A Quote by Karen E. Quinones Miller. (n.d.). Retrieved September 23, 2015, from http://www.goodreads.com/quotes/145516-when-someone-tells-me-no-it-doesn-t-mean-i-can-t

I have spent a big part of my life as a professional photographer. I got hooked when I was 16 years old, and since then I have shot just about everything you could photograph. I have done it full-time and part-time on and off throughout my career. Over 35 years, I have had thousands of clients. I'm a very accomplished photographer.

My problem used to be that I was so insecure and worried about what other people thought of me that I spent my life doubting myself as a photographer and whatever else I was doing. I had a deep desire to impress my two elder brothers, who were 10 and 11 years older me. All I wanted was to impress them and get some praise from them. I wanted this more than anything.

A few years ago, we had a family gathering, and I gathered the nerve to approach my brothers and show them my portfolio. It was my best work, and I just wanted some praise. As I showed it to them, they did nothing but shoot it down, make fun of every picture, and tease me in a brotherly way. I went back into the house, threw the portfolio against the wall, and cried uncontrollably.

At that point, I made up my mind to quit photography, even though I had thousands of clients who loved my work. The toxic people in my life at that time were my own brothers. Since I believed every word they said, I had a hard time picking up the camera again. So be careful whom you share your goals and dreams with.

You have a choice to make about conquering your fear and trusting yourself. I can't make it for you, and nobody in your support group can make it for you either. You can throw in the towel right now, or you can use that towel to wipe away the sweat off your face from working so hard to find the real you. Stop now and think about fear and trust in your life.

Remember: It's all about taking extremely small steps to achieve your long-term goal and ambition. It could, for example, be a decision to spend today being as positive as you can. You could decide to spend the day thinking and talking to yourself about your goals and dreams. You could try and see how long you can stay positive for the next couple of days. It could be a 15-minute goal, an hourly goal, or a half-day or full-day goal. If you can do it for a day, then you can do it for two days. Whatever your goal is, write it down today. Remember constant small steps are the key.

Chapter 5

Key 3: Moving from Darkness to Light

In the last chapter, we talked about trusting yourself being the foundation for getting better and making changes. In this chapter, I want to discuss moving from darkness to light.

Let's return to the question I posed at the beginning of the book: How long do you want to stay the way you are right now? Hopefully, you have answered that question as you have written your goals.

When I answered that question, my response was not so much a timetable. I just didn't want to be the way I was one day longer than I had to. Like many of you, I had spent a lot of my life in the darkness of depression. I had lived my life looking through a dark and foggy filter that drained the life out of everything.

As I began moving from darkness to light, I felt like I had spent my life in a giant dark room. I knew that there was a light switch somewhere, but I also knew that nobody was going to flip that switch for me. Though there were vast amounts of electricity, it wasn't going to turn on by itself. It was my job to find it.

Over the years and by taking small steps, I found the light switch, and I was able to flip it. However, flipping the switch didn't make everything in my life perfect. It was a daily process. It was as if the switch had a dimmer on it, and the light was there, but it was very weak at first. As I continued to work on being positive, setting small goals, and noticing and celebrating moments in my life, the light got brighter.

Conquer the Darkness

When I was a child, I loved light. Whenever my parents would go away for the evening, I would turn on every light in the house because it made me less scared of being alone.

At a young age, we were all taught the physical law that light and darkness cannot occupy the same place at the same time; when the light comes, darkness leaves.

You have a choice in your life: You can allow your past to defeat you, overwhelm you, paralyze you, and make you quit. Or you can empower your past and turn the pain, anguish, heartache, and darkness into a compelling weapon to use in the war against being miserable.

Bestselling author Dr. Steve Maraboli said: "Fear can only grow in darkness. Once you face fear with light, you win."[25] Many of us have spent such a long time in a room or a tunnel where there is no light that we believe that there is no light switch. We think it's just a place of evil darkness, but that is not true. I know that if you believe that there is a light switch, there will be one, and you will be able to flip that switch. Take a minute and think about how it will feel to flip that switch.

In the last chapter, I mentioned that you must get the toxic people around you out of your life because all they do is feed your darkness and make it worse. You also need to find what I call angels for lack of a better word. The angels were sent to earth to help you, support you, and love you no matter what. These are your friends, your family, and perhaps even people you haven't met yet.

---

[25] A Quote from Life, the Truth, and Being Free. (n.d.). Retrieved September 23, 2015, from https://www.goodreads.com/quotes/318960-fear-can-only-grow-in-darkness-once-you-face-fear

While I was battling the darkness, I had people in my life who knew everything I was going through. They knew my pain, my fears, my sorrows, and my struggles. They didn't always understand them, but they knew all about me, and they still loved me. They cared about me and were there for me whenever I needed them. They were my angels.

When we get the flu or a cold, we easily seek help from other people and throw a little pity party. We want people to take care of us and make us feel better. When we have mental difficulties, we are reluctant to admit it. We don't want anybody to know how we are and what is going on in our lives. It is a stigma that comes with having mental challenges that we need to get past. You need to find those angels – that support system in your life.

Dealing with depression, anxiety, and panic and being unfulfilled in our life is exhausting. We have to work much harder than others just to get through the day. At work, I would have presentations and speeches that I would have to give. Just putting in the energy for that hour or so seemed like it would take a week's worth of energy out of me, and I was fighting to survive the rest of the week.

Fatigue is a common enemy of us all. Religious leader Jeffrey R. Holland said that we need to "slow down, rest up, replenish, and refill."[26] He continues: "Physicians promise us that if we do not take time to be well, we most assuredly will take time later on to be ill."[27] We must not overdo it. That is why I talk about small steps. The process of recovery is not a marathon; it's a journey. It won't happen overnight.

I hope and pray that with these keys that I am giving you, it won't take you as long as it took me. I had to start from scratch and find my

---

[26] Holland, J. R. (2013, October). *Like a Broken Vessel*. Retrieved September 23, 2015, from https://www.lds.org/general-conference/2013/10/like-a-broken-vessel?lang=eng

[27] Holland, J. R. (2013, October). *Like a Broken Vessel*. Retrieved September 23, 2015, from https://www.lds.org/general-conference/2013/10/like-a-broken-vessel?lang=eng

path. I hope that by sharing these keys and examples with you, it doesn't take as long for you to flip your switch and find your miracle.

We wear ourselves out and get tired because we keep asking ourselves "When will I feel better?" "When am I going to feel happy?" "What if I never feel better again?" We need to concentrate on the light bulb moments – the little positive things that happen every day – and not the things that cause us to be anxious and panic, which fills us with darkness and depression.

I wish there were a way for me to meet each of you, talk to you, and get to know you. I would want to let you know the astonishing light that is inside you, your real you, your inner self, and the amazing things that God, the Universe, or a Higher Power has in store for you.

I love the Olympics. One of the first things they do at the Olympics is light the Olympic flame. During the event, the flame never goes out – it always burns. You need to make a decision to light a flame of your own that never goes out. Many of you already have a flame inside. Though it might be just a small flame, you can make it bigger, and it can be with you and help you through your journey.

Religious leader Robert D. Hales tells a story of when he was younger:

When I was a boy, I used to ride my bicycle home from basketball practice at night. I would connect a small pear-shaped generator to my bicycle tire. Then as I pedaled, the tire would turn a tiny rotor, which produced electricity and emitted a single, welcome beam of light. [...] I learned quickly that if I stopped pedaling my bicycle, the light would go out. I also learned that when I was "anxiously engaged" in pedaling, the light would become brighter, and the darkness in front of me would be dispelled.[28]

---

[28] Hales, R. D. (2002, April). *Out of Darkness into His Marvelous Light.* Retrieved September 23, 2015, from https://www.lds.org/general-conference/2002/04/out-of-darkness-into-his-marvelous-light?lang=eng

We need to be pedaling forward and not backward daily. We need to keep that steady, persistent energy while pedaling, and we will see that the darkness can't be where there is light.

Muhammad Ali is one of my favorite people and someone I look up to. He used to make predictions about what was going to happen in his next fight. Most of the time, his predictions came true. He said: "A rooster crows only when it sees the light. Put him in the dark and he'll never crow. I have seen the light and I'm crowing."[29] Through the Seven Essential Keys, I have learned how to crow. Now it's your turn to crow!

Look for the Rainbows in Your Life

We need to look for the rainbows, the bright spots, or the light bulb moments in our lives. When our lives are filled with darkness, we will see life in black and white, and the joy, the beauty, and the colors fade away. When we reduce our lives to black and white, we will never see rainbows.

Financial services executive J.P. Morgan said: "The first step towards getting somewhere is to decide that you are not going to stay where you are."[30] Making a decision to move forward is what I have talked about the last few chapters. There will be failures, and there will be trials. Difficult things will happen, but you have to persist and keep going. Stop and think about where you want to go in life.

I have found that the greater the storm I face, the brighter is the rainbow that I find. My life is not perfect, but there is light, trust, and faith. There are colors, beauty, and happiness. I have found a way to control the darkness, the fear, the panic, and the anxiety. I no longer suffer as much from those things, and they don't control my life; I control them.

---

[29]   Muhammad Ali Quote. (n.d.). Retrieved September 23, 2015, from http://www.brainyquote.com/quotes/quotes/m/muhammadal167375.html

[30]   A Quote by J.P. Morgan. (n.d.). Retrieved September 23, 2015, from http://www.goodreads.com/quotes/223825-the-first-step-towards-getting-somewhere-is-to-decide-that

At the beginning of the book, I encouraged you to write down your dreams and goals. If you haven't taken the time or the chance to do that yet, I ask you to stop reading right now and do it. This is one of the main keys to getting better. Don't let the fear win. Let your dreams and goals flow and write them down. Write down what you want to accomplish short-term, mid-term, and long-term.

I understand depression. I was bipolar, so I know that it can be difficult to set a goal. It might feel impossible to think about things in the future and have hope, but hope is one thing we always have when everything else is tough.

Everybody wants to be happy; nobody wants to have pain and misery in life. But you can't have a rainbow without a little bit of rain. Storms will come, but every time you beat one, you become stronger and more positive, and you are going to believe in yourself more. As you become increasingly more positive, the people around you will become more positive as well. When you receive more help, the people around you, your support system, will become more hopeful. The Universe and God will put people in your life, angels as I call them, who will help you get better.

Sit down and brainstorm your goals. You can't simply say, "I just want these things to happen." The act of writing them down makes your powerful subconscious mind start to look for a way to make them happen.

There are two important things I want you to keep in mind here. First, make sure the goals you set aren't impossible but achievable. If you set a goal that is unreasonable and extremely difficult to accomplish, you never will reach it. If you don't reach it, it will have a negative effect on your life, and it will decrease your confidence. Also, resist the urge to set goals that don't take much effort to accomplish. This was the hardest thing I had to do, and it was the greatest thing I could ever do for myself.

Set deadlines for your goals. You can always move the deadline. Moving it doesn't mean you have failed. When you work on a deadline, you become more urgent, and you will achieve your goal more quickly. A goal that is not written down is only a wish. You need to get busy and start thinking about it.

Learn to count your rainbows – your golden light bulb moments – through this journey. Don't count the thunderstorms – the failures and challenges that come. They will come, but that just means you're being successful in the journey.

When it comes to your angels, some of you already have them around you, and you know who they are. They are people who you can count on. One of these people in my life is one of my best friends, Bryan. We have been friends for about 16 years. There is nothing he doesn't know about my struggle. I have shared everything with him.

Very early in our friendship, I went to him and said:

"I need a few people in my life that I can count on when I'm depressed and suicidal. I need someone who I can call 24 hours a day, whenever I need somebody to be there for me. If you don't want to do that, that's fine because I would need a commitment from you."

"Absolutely," he replied.

Since then, he has been there for me whenever I have needed him. Sometimes, it has been late at night. Other times, it has been early in the morning. Sometimes, it has been inconvenient for him. But God and the Universe put him in my life, three doors down the street, to help me through some of the hardest times in my life. He is one of my angels.

As you continue to go through the process and get better, people are put in your life. A few years ago, I went to a therapist who I only saw once. She could see that I had tried everything and that I was extremely discouraged. I was so down that she was scared to have me leave her office.

She then made a suggestion that brought about the miracle that changed my life. Not only did it save my life, but it also changed it in unbelievable ways. I will tell you more about this miracle at the end of this book.

Several months later, I went back to the therapist after that miracle had happened to thank her for being an angel in my life. She couldn't believe how much I had changed. She was amazed by how big my smile was and how fulfilled my life was. We hugged and cried.

I don't know what your miracle will be. It might not be the same as mine, but perhaps it will be. It could be your support system. It could be medication. It could be a book. It could be therapy. Or it could be another of the unbelievable things that are out there just for you.

Whenever you find yourself doubting if you can go on, just remember how far you have come. Remember everything you have faced, all the battles you have won, and all the fears that you have overcome. Remember your 100% success rate. Then raise your head high and forge on ahead knowing that you have got this and that you are going to succeed.

Chapter 6
Key 4: Serving Others

Now we will talk about the fourth key, which is serving others. It's a bit of a change from what we have discussed earlier. Up until now, we have talked about taking care of you and making changes to yourself. However, one of the major things in life is to focus on helping other people. In return, it helps us to heal more quickly.

Gandhi said: "The best way to find yourself is to lose yourself in the service of others."[31] Through my journey, I found that to be true. When I could focus on helping other people, even with a small gesture like a smile or a hug, I was blessed.

Depression, anxiety, fear, and all those things that we have talked about create feelings of hopelessness. The simple cure for hopelessness is hope. Hope is the one thing that we can never lose through this journey. Focusing on others while you're trying to take care of yourself is a good balance. The outward focus brings more hope into your being and helps you work through the challenges that come with mental illness.

The world that we live in sometimes teaches the opposite of that. There are a lot of blogs, magazines, TV shows, books, and other forms of media that tell you how to live your life, how to be rich, and how

---

[31] Mahatma Gandhi Quote. (n.d.). Retrieved September 23, 2015, from http://www.brainyquote.com/quotes/quotes/m/mahatmagan150725.html

to get more out of life. What they do is they teach you to focus only on yourself and make yourself better. They guide you to set goals for yourself and not worry about anybody but yourself. It's a very selfish way of going about life.

We see on TV, in the newspapers, and on different social media outlets people pursuing power. Some people will be ruthless and do whatever they can to get power, no matter how many people they hurt. They climb the ladder of success. When they reach the top after they have devoted their whole lives to their selfish ambitions, they find that the ladder of success was up against the wrong wall. They find themselves successful but miserable, lonely, and unfulfilled because there is nobody with whom they can share their success. I'm sure you know or have worked for someone like this.

Helping others is one of the doors to recovery that you have to open. We have already discussed other doors such as the door from darkness to light, the door of fear, the door of believing in yourself, and the door of knowing that God and the Universe will not give you more than you can handle.

A Good Deed Brightens a Dark World

We all come from a dark world, but good deeds bring light into that dark world. By doing good deeds for other people and yourself, God, the Universe, or a Higher Being – whatever you believe in – will send back light into your life. The darkness in your life will begin to flee and leave. I have seen it happen in my life over the years, so I know it's true. I know that serving others was one of the keys that helped me beat my depression, smile, and turn my life around.

If you give to other people, it lowers stress in your life. That is not the reason we do it, but it's a law of the Universe that you get more back than you ever give and that giving to others increases your happiness.

Jim Rohn, one of my favorite speakers, said: "Only by giving are you able to receive more than you already have."[32] You can give continuously, and you will never run out because you receive so much in return.

Say you had a freezer full of roasts, steaks, and very expensive cuts of meat, and you constantly kept handing these to people. But every time to you went back to the freezer, it was full again. In the same way, when you do good to others, you never run out because those blessings come back to you all the time – the freezer is always full of meat no matter how much you give away.

There is a thing that we call karma. Most of the time, we think of karma as a negative thing. What goes around comes around. Karma is going to get you in the future. It works both ways. If you do bad, the Universe is going to send bad things to you. But if you are a kind person, and you help people, good things are going to happen to you.

The notion of karma changes your perspective on life. You see that when you do good deeds, you receive good things back from the Universe. You feel better about yourself when helping other people, and you start to be more positive. You start having faith and hope that the next thing that happens in your life is going to be positive one rather than negative. Karma is amazing!

Mohammed Ali said: "Service to others is the rent you pay for your room here on earth."[33] We pay back God and the Universe by serving others. One of my favorite religious leaders, Gordon B. Hinckley, said: "tremendous happiness […] comes of service to others. […] No man can live fully and happily who lives only unto himself."[34]

---

[32] A Quote by Jim Rohn. (n.d.). Retrieved September 23, 2015, from http://www.goodreads.com/quotes/718488-only-by-giving-are-you-able-to-receive-more-than

[33] Muhammad Ali Quote. (n.d.). Retrieved September 23, 2015, from http://www.brainyquote.com/quotes/quotes/m/muhammadal136676.html

[34] Hinckley, G. B. (1992, August 1). I Believe. Retrieved September 23, 2015, from https://www.lds.org/ensign/1992/08/i-believe?lang=eng

Earlier, I told you about the death of our son, Connor. The day we found out that Connor had passed away in Taiwan, 7,000 miles away from where we were, was the worst day of my life. It was also one of the most unbelievable days of service ever given to our family.

We found out at midnight that Connor had died. The word started to get out and at about 7:00 in the morning, people started coming to our house. We have a very close-knit neighborhood and a very close-knit church family, and as people heard what had happened, they all started to come. By late morning, we had to move outside on our front lawn because there were too many people for us all to be in the house. All day long till about 10:00 or 11:00 that night, we had between 50 and 100 people at our house constantly. They were serving us and brought us food and flowers, hugs and tears, and anything they could. I quickly learned how therapeutic hugs were.

At about noon, Connor's death became a news story on the Internet, and then things exploded. The phone calls came from friends, relatives, and people who hadn't heard yet. Since we live in Utah, and he was a missionary from here, it was a big deal.

At about 1:00 pm, as the news channels started to call our family looking for comments, it began to bother my wife and me. We decided to do a news conference with all of the TV stations and newspapers at one time. As soon as we told the people in our front yard that we were going to do a news conference at our house two hours hence, the people who didn't know what to do because they were grieving had a chance to serve. One person looked at me and asked, "Where's your lawnmower?" Another person asked, "Where's the tools to rake your lawn?" And then someone asked for a chainsaw. All of a sudden, they were dozens of people working on our lawn, our trees, our bushes, and our house. They all wanted the house to look beautiful for the news conference. We were speechless.

It gave the ones who didn't know what to do a chance to serve. They wept, and they brought flower arrangements and pots to put them in.

Somebody even brought a beautiful bench. I left to be in my office for 30 minutes to write our family statement for the press. When I came back, I couldn't believe the difference they had made to our house. Tears welled up in my eyes because of how they served us. Each one of them received blessings for their service. A senior missionary couple worked in our backyard for three days. They said: "Just let us work. That's how we're dealing with this. We grieve by helping." Winston Churchill said: "We make a living by what we get, but we make a life by what we give."[35] Take a minute and think about the amount of giving you are doing in your life.

An Exercise Crazy World

We live in an exercise crazy world. People are exercising and doing a lot of different things to get healthy. I'm not one of those people. I love to walk with my wife and our dog. The best exercise for a happy life is not jumping jacks, push-ups, crunches, squats, lunges, or running. The best exercise for a happy life is service. Religious leader Thomas S. Monson said:

> Those who live only for themselves eventually shrivel up and figuratively lose their lives, while those who lose themselves in service to others grow and flourish — and in effect save their lives.[36]

That's what this book is about — saving and transforming your life, finding your purpose, and moving yourself from darkness to light.

Exercise means getting off the couch and out of that dark room. It makes us stronger. That is what serving other people does. It makes us stronger mentally, and that is essential when we deal with mental challenges. It helps us deal with stress better. When you are out, and you

---

[35] Winston Churchill Quote. (n.d.). Retrieved September 23, 2015, from http://www.brainyquote.com/quotes/quotes/w/winstonchu131192.html

[36] A Quote by Thomas S. Monson. (n.d.). Retrieved September 23, 2015, from https://www.goodreads.com/quotes/273458-i-believe-the-savior-is-telling-us-that-unless-we

are busy taking care of things, it lowers your anxiety and stress level, which helps us live longer.

Helping and serving others will move your attention away from your own problems. You're not focused on you. Sometimes we get in such a rut that we can't see anything but our own problems. Then we just sit day after day and look for a way to get out of the rut that we are in. Helping others breaks that cycle. It helps us think clearer and smarter and make better decisions. As you assist in healing other people's wounds, your wounds will heal faster.

It's karma; when you help other people heal, you will heal. It's a law of the Universe – a law of God. I've seen it in my life. I've been extremely depressed and felt overcome and crushed by darkness and lack of hope in my life. During those times, other people have pushed me, and I have gone to serve and help, whether by cleaning up a yard, helping somebody move or many different forms of service. For that entire time, I would be laughing and joking, and none of that darkness would be with me. The minute I would get home, I would start thinking about myself again, and it would all come back. But the time I was out, I would be focused on somebody else and their needs, so it was a blessing.

Gordon B. Hinckley also said:

The best antidote I know for worry is work. The best cure for weariness is the challenge of helping someone who is even more tired. One of the great ironies of life is this: He or she who serves almost always benefits more than he or she who is served.[37]

The great educator Booker T. Washington said: "If you want to lift yourself up, lift up someone else."[38] All these great leaders and teachers

[37] A Quote from Standing for Something. (n.d.). Retrieved September 23, 2015, from http://www.goodreads.com/quotes/31208-the-best-antidote-i-know-for-worry-is-work-the

[38] Booker T. Washington Quote. (n.d.). Retrieved September 23, 2015, from http://www.brainyquote.com/quotes/quotes/b/bookertwa382202.html

throughout history are telling us why we are on this earth – what our purpose is. Our purpose is to learn and grow, to help others, and to learn to love and trust life.

One warning that I want to give when it comes to helping or serving others is that we need to keep it in balance. If we volunteer and help others too much, we can neglect ourselves. There is a balance that we need to keep between focusing on helping ourselves and taking the time to help other people. Don't set your goals too high; you can't fix the whole world's problems. You can't take somebody's major problems and carry them yourself. Those are their problems, but you can help and be a support to them, just like you have people who support you.

As my wife and I went through the experience with the loss of our son and the unbelievable acts of service, care, and love, we made ourselves busy to work through our grief. We began serving other people and focusing our energy and grief on helping others.

During that same week that our son died, our neighbor around the corner also experienced a tragedy. My sons used to work for this man in his construction business. His daughter fell down a flight of stairs in her home and hit her head on the concrete floor. She went into a coma and died several days after my son. She had four little boys under the age of seven. We tried to be there for them, so we went to the visitation and funeral, and we did everything we could for them.

An elderly gentleman, who lived two houses down from us, passed away that same week. We wanted to be there for his wife and his children, so we visited his wife and attended the funeral.

We had also been invited to a wedding that took place a week after our son died. We went, and a lot of people were surprised that we were there. To partake in this joyous and happy occasion where this beautiful young couple got married was good for us. And it was great to be there for them. We took our eyes off ourselves. We were comforted, and we received blessings down the road from doing that service.

A few days after our son Connor died, some teenage girls from our church brought dinner to our house. We invited them to sit and talk with us because we could see they were scared. They had gone to school and been friends with my son, and they had never lost anybody that close to them before, so they were scared. They had questions. "Why do bad things happen to good people?" They wondered. They also wondered about heaven and hell and where we believed that Connor was. We talked to them, and we shared and we gave from our hearts. It was strengthening for us to serve these young girls and to help strengthen them and their faith.

One way we can focus outward is by helping others who suffer from the same thing we do. In Alcoholics Anonymous, the sponsors have been alcoholics, and they work with someone who is dealing with that same disease. I sought out the leader of my church and asked him if there were other people who dealt with depression that I could be a resource to. I also volunteered and worked at a hospital, and I went to the psychiatric unit and met with people who were depressed and lonely just to be a support for them.

There are also little things you can do. You can give someone a hug. Hugs are unbelievably powerful. It could be the only expression of love that a person receives all day. It could be a smile to a stranger. You might be the only sunshine in somebody's life that day. I love to open doors for older people and smile. Sometimes their response is: "Do you know how many years it's been since a young man opened the door for me?"

Whatever kind of service you do, giving to others is important in your process of getting better. The world renowned artist Picasso said: "The meaning of life is to find your gift. The purpose of life is to give it away."[39]

---

[39] A Quote by Pablo Picasso. (n.d.). Retrieved September 23, 2015, from http://www.goodreads.com/quotes/607827-the-meaning-of-life-is-to-find-your-gift-the

Chapter 7
Key 5: Persistence

"If you can't fly then run, if you can't run then walk, if you can't walk then crawl, but whatever you do you have to keep moving forward."[40]

—Dr. Martin Luther King, Jr.

Small steps can turn into large steps. What is important is that we keep moving forward. We have to be in the present; we have to be in today. Today is a special day, and that is why they call it the present. We need to be in the present and not the past, and we need to look toward the future.

Years ago, I saw *Star Wars: Return of the Jedi* together with my kids. In the movie, there is a scene where Luke's X-wing star fighter has sunk into the lake.

Luke says to Yoda: "Oh no, I'll never get it know."

Yoda stamps his foot, gets angry, and says: "So certain are you, always with you what cannot be done. Hear you nothing that I say?"

Luke looks hopelessly out at his ship and says: "Master, moving stones around is one thing. This is totally different."

"No! No different. Only different in your mind. You must unlearn what you have learned," Yoda replies.

---

[40] A Quote by Martin Luther King, Jr. (n.d.). Retrieved September 23, 2015, from http://www.goodreads.com/quotes/26963-if-you-can-t-fly-then-run-if-you-can-t-run

Luke looks out at his sunken X-wing star fighter and says: "Alright, I'll give it a try."

"No! Try not. Do. Or do not. There is no try," says Yoda.[41]

I remembered that scene for years through my depression. And I have repeated it to a lot of people. There is do or do not, but there is no try. We have all heard the adage "If at first you don't succeed, try and try again." That is a good thought, but it's not quite right; it's not the whole truth. To try means to attempt something. It does not necessarily mean a commitment to succeed. Saying "It might work, and it might not, but I'll try," is a lot different than saying "I'm going to keep at it until I win, and I'm not going to fail." In the past, you have probably said, "Well, I'll try," while thinking that you probably won't succeed but do the best you can. If you want to get better, you have to make a commitment. Tell yourself out loud right now that you will not try, you will do it.

While I was in the psychiatric unit at the hospital in Phoenix, I decided that I was not going to be in and out of psychiatric units my whole life. I was determined to do whatever I could no matter how long it would take to get better. I made that commitment that day. I wasn't going to try; I was going to do it. And I did it.

We are only confined by the walls that we built around ourselves. Our fear, anxiety, and lack of faith that we can do it are all that hold us back. In the Bible, the word "try" appears 83 times. In most of those cases and stories, every first attempt was an unsuccessful or half-hearted effort. We have a big challenge ahead of us. We have tough things to beat to achieve mental health. And a lot of them are life and death situations to some of us.

We need to make a commitment that we are not just going to try; we're going to do it. If we just try, we will quit when we encounter the first obstacle that shows up. If we are determined, and we make a

---

41 *Yoda-ism's - Words to Live By.* (n.d.). Retrieved September 23, 2015, from
    http://www.destinationhollywood.com/movies/starwars/moviequotes_yoda.shtml

commitment, we are going to find a way to go over, under, around, or through the obstacles. It's just going to be one little step that you have to take to get past the obstacle and move on to the next one. Remember that obstacles and failures are parts of success.

I love this quote by Winston Churchill: "If you're going through hell, keep going."[42] I was in hell for 40 years, and I kept going through it. I was in it for a lot longer than I hope you have to be. Things have improved over the last 40 years. Support systems have become stronger, medications have improved, and the flux of information is better. You can use the seven steps that I'm showing you in this book that I had to find by myself. So it shouldn't take you as long as it took me. But it's going to take as long as it does, and that depends on you and your commitment to getting better.

We need to have self-discipline – the ability to get ourselves to take actions regardless of where we are emotionally. It's like a muscle; if you train the muscle, it will get stronger. And the less you train it, it will weaken. Each of us has different muscle strength. We also have different levels of self-discipline. It takes self-discipline to build self-discipline. You have to take those steps every day and work at it every day – even the bad days when you wake up unmotivated and that night go to bed discouraged. Then you should go to bed telling yourself, "I'll try again tomorrow. Today was a tough day." You must wake up with determination and go to bed with satisfaction. You need to be satisfied with your efforts because that time is gone. You also need to see the positive. Consider how far you have moved along, even if it is only a step because it is still positive. Consistent small steps are the key.

One of the scariest things that any of us can do is to quit before the blessings come. Byrd Baggett said, "Don't quit before the blessing."[43]

---

[42] Winston Churchill Quote. (n.d.). Retrieved September 23, 2015, from http://www.brainyquote.com/quotes/quotes/w/winstonchu103788.html

[43] Don't Quit Before the Blessing Desktop Wallpaper | Byrd Baggett. (n.d.). Retrieved September 23, 2015, from http://www.byrdbaggett.com/free/wallpapers/dqbtb2.php

When everything is going wrong, and you feel like you can't take it one more day — that is usually when the light is going to come.

I searched for 40 years for the miracle that I will tell you about at the end of this book. When it came, I was at one of the lowest points that I had been in 40 years. I was tired, and I didn't want to try anymore. I had no any energy left. My faith was gone, and I was losing hope. But I didn't give up, and then it happened. If I had given up one day earlier, it wouldn't have happened.

Constant small steps make a huge progression and getting little things done make big things happen. Say you get 1% better at beating your depression, anxiety, or panic every week. One percent is not very much. Since I'm a nice guy, I'll give you two weeks where you don't have to become 1% better. If you do that, you will become 50% better within one year. That is a huge accomplishment. Just by persistently getting 1% better every week for a year, with two weeks' vacation, you would be 50% better at what you chose to get better at.

Calvin Coolidge, former president of the United States, said:

Nothing in this world can take the place of persistence. Talent will not: nothing is more common than unsuccessful men with talent. Genius will not; unrewarded genius is almost a proverb. Education will not: the world is full of educated derelicts. Persistence and determination alone are omnipotent.[44]

He also said, "The slogan 'Press On' has solved and always will solve the problems of the human race."[45]

---

[44] Calvin Coolidge Quote. (n.d.). Retrieved September 23, 2015, from http://www.brainyquote.com/quotes/quotes/c/calvincool414555.html

[45] Calvin Coolidge Quote. (n.d.). Retrieved September 23, 2015, from http://www.brainyquote.com/quotes/quotes/c/calvincool414555.html

Remember the "Why"

We need to remember why we are trying to get better. We must remember it when we get discouraged, when we have a bad day, when we feel like we're going backward, and when we think it's never going to happen. We need to remember why we are doing it.

What is your "why"? When you feel like giving up, remember why you held on so long in the first place. Whatever you do, do not give up. It is all about your goal. The name written on the victory over these mental challenges is yours. It's nobody else's; this is your fight.

When I went through my challenges, I was looking for people who understood what these challenges were like. I knew it could only be people who were going through the same thing as me. I remember getting on an online chat forum for depressed people. It was once a week, and it was enjoyable. We helped each other, and there was a moderator who was there to keep us on task and keep us talking about positive things.

Originally, there were six of us. A few months later, I noticed that there were five of us. And then another few months later, there were four of us. I thought they were just not there for a couple of weeks. Then there were three of us. And there were two of us. Eventually, after over a year and a half, there were just the moderator and me. One Thursday night, I asked him, "Where is everybody?" Then he told me that they had all given up and committed suicide. That was devastating for me, but it made me try even harder.

Never give up. You need to remember why you are fighting to get better. You are doing it for yourself, God, the Universe, or whatever that Higher Power is for you. Then you are doing it for your spouse, parents, kids, friends, etc. Don't give up. Find your role model and draw inspiration from that person. It could be one of the successful people we talked about at the beginning of the book, or it could be someone else who has beaten it. Draw inspiration from that person. Don't let your past failures haunt you. Gain confidence from your failures. The more failures you have, the closer you are to reaching your goal.

Self-Determination

Nobody is going to win the battle for you. You have a support system, but they are not going to do it for you. Self-determination is what will constantly get you moving forward towards your goals rather than away from them. Self-determination helps you to keep moving forward no matter how hard it gets. Even on the days when you're not motivated to do anything at all, the determination will keep you moving. It helps you to overcome negative habits and negative thinking.

Self-determination helps you to go back to the "why" – what you wrote down about the amazing life you're going to live, your purpose in life, the things you want to accomplish. Self-determination will keep you going even when everybody and everything around you are telling you to quit and give up. At that point, you still believe that what you're doing is going to work because you have that inner self-determination and belief.

Author Robert Collier said: "Success is the sum of small efforts – repeated day in and day out."[46] Harriet Beecher Stowe who wrote Uncle Tom's Cabin said:

> When you get into a tight space and everything goes against you, till it seems as though you could not hang on a minute longer, never give up then, for that is just the place and time that the tide will turn.[47]

It was at that moment that my miracle happened. I was at the bottom. This miracle that I had is nicknamed "The Last Chance." It is what you do when you have tried everything else.

---

[46] Robert Collier Quote. (n.d.). Retrieved September 23, 2015, from http://www.brainyquote.com/quotes/quotes/r/robertcoll108959.html

[47] Harriet Beecher Stowe Quote. (n.d.). Retrieved September 23, 2015, from http://www.brainyquote.com/quotes/quotes/h/harrietbee126390.html

Now let me warn you: Sometimes, if the road you are going down and the things you are trying aren't working, giving up may be the best option. Let me explain. I told you about the therapist I went to whom I didn't click with. I made the decision not to go to that therapist anymore. I didn't believe or trust what he taught. It wasn't that it was incorrect; it just wasn't for me. When it came to medications, I was the one who made the decision to go to the doctor and say: "I don't want to be on this medication anymore." I didn't like how it makes me feel and what it makes me do, so I made that decision. Some of the books I started to read I didn't like, so I stopped. Sometimes we need to change up how we're getting there.

Have you have heard of a company called Traf-O-Data? I never had. But have you ever heard of Microsoft? Bill Gates and Paul Allen started both companies. Traf-O-Data was the first company that Bill Gates and Paul Allen started back in 1972. They ran it for several years, and then they threw in the towel and said it wasn't working. They gave up on it. Then they started a tiny little company called Microsoft. Sometimes giving up on something that is not working to try something else is the right move.

I want to close this chapter with a story that, to be honest with you, I'm embarrassed to tell you. But I want to get across the point of never giving up.

About three years ago, my wife and I found out we were going to have our first granddaughter. To most people to be told that they will become grandparents is an amazing and exciting thing to hear. I remember sitting down with one of my church leaders getting counseling, and he was very excited for me because he was a grandfather, so he already knew the incredible feelings and emotions that this new chapter of life brings.

I looked at him, and I said: "It's not fair for this little girl to have me as a grandfather because I'm so depressed and angry and moody. I'm not a happy person to be around. I have set a goal to kill myself before she is born so that she doesn't have to deal with a grouchy grandfather." I came very closely to making that goal come true.

But now I can't put into words the joy and the blessing this little girl is in my life. I can't describe what I would have missed if I had given up and never had the chance to see her. And now she has a little brother who I love just as much.

Another church leader once saw me playing with my grandkids when they were sitting on my lap during the church service. After the service, he came back towards me and said: "In all the years I have known you, I have never seen you happier than you are playing with your grandchildren. Never have I seen you smile that big."

Writer Jim Watkins said: "A river cuts through a rock, not because of its power but its persistence."[48]

48 Pollock, M. (n.d.). *28 Inspiring Quotes About Perseverance and Persistence.* Retrieved September 23, 2015, from http://www.michaeldpollock.com/inspiring-quotes-persistence-perseverance/

Chapter 8
Key 6: Patience

In this chapter, I want to talk about the sixth key, which is patience. For many, having patience is hard because it's something that has to be learned. It can be very bitter, but the fruits and rewards of it are very sweet.

Tolstoy said: "The strongest of all warriors are these two – Time and Patience."[49] Fighting to beat mental illness takes both time and patience. Discovering the real you, the person that God and the Universe want you to be, and learning to use the talents that you were given also takes time. You will encounter many challenges and failures. However, as long as you are pointed in the right direction, and you keep moving forward, you will eventually get there.

Patience is learning to wait and live with the challenges you have. It's knowing that these challenges will someday be gone if you believe in yourself and have faith that you can go from darkness to light. Even if you can only do that a part of the day, it's still moving you in the right direction.

Unfortunately, we live in a world where everything is about instant gratification. Technology makes everything available immediately, and credit cards allow us to buy things with money we haven't even earned yet. As a result, many are brought up to be impatient. People don't want to wait and have no desire to be patient.

---

49   A Quote from War and Peace. (n.d.). Retrieved September 23, 2015, from https://www.goodreads.com/quotes/239082-the-strongest-of-all-warriors-are-these-two-time

This journey is going to be more difficult if you're an impatient person because God and the Universe have a perfect timing. Things will not happen when we want them to but at the time that is perfect for us. I certainly didn't want to wait 40 years. When my miracle finally happened, I had dealt with depression, anxiety, panic, and low self-esteem 80% of my life.

If you have a habit of being impatient, you have to break that habit. You also have to believe in the Universe or God and believe that your miracle will happen, but it's going to happen at the perfect time for you. Stop now and think about the habit of being patient.

Another challenge that comes with learning patience is that you have to have patience to be patient. Learning to be patient takes patience. Shakespeare said: "To climb steep hills requires a slow pace at first."[50] You have to take the small steps that we have discussed daily and reward yourself when you have little victories and accomplish your goals.

Right in front of my house, I can see a 10,000-foot mountain. If I were to start running up that mountain as fast as I could, I wouldn't get very far before I would be exhausted, and I would have to turn around and quit. It takes several hours, sometimes half a day, to climb this mountain. You have to start slow and keep a constant pace to get to the top of the mountain. It is the same thing with using these keys, your support group, your medical group, and all those things we have discussed that work together to help you get there. But you are the one who has to take the steps. You're the one who has to climb the hill.

When I say patience, I don't mean waiting for a magic thing to happen without doing anything, and then suddenly you will be better. That is never going to happen. Patience is doing something about the situation that you're in and knowing that the result is going to come down the road. I don't know when your miracle will come, and I don't

---

[50] A Quote by William Shakespeare. (n.d.). Retrieved September 23, 2015, from http://www.goodreads.com/quotes/30651-to-climb-steep-hills-requires-a-slow-pace-at-first

know what it's going to be. It could be entirely different from mine. I do know that by using these keys that we are discussing, it will happen for you if it's supposed to happen.

Another thing that we need is discipline to work along with our patience. We need the discipline to work toward our goal every day regardless of how we feel. Regardless of whether we feel positive or negative, we need to have the discipline to use the tools that I give you in this book. The author Thomas M. Sterner said: "The problem with patience and discipline is that it requires both of them to develop each of them."[51] You already have to have the patience to be patient. You have to have some discipline to be disciplined.

The three keys to this that we have talked about in three of the previous chapters are what author Napoleon Hill captured in this quote: "Patience, persistence and perspiration make an unbeatable combination for success."[52] That means working like you have never worked in your life because there is nothing more important than your life, becoming the person that the Universe or God wants you to be, and serving and helping other people along the way.

Earlier I talked about toxic people. Unfortunately, my most powerful example was my brothers. If you remember, they teased me about my photography portfolio, which was one of my most cherished possessions. I was very proud of it, so their feedback destroyed me emotionally and mentally.

One night, as I was learning more about myself and being patient and serving other people, my wife said: "You need to forgive your brothers for everything they said. You carry around this grudge. You

---

[51] A Quote by Thomas M. Sterner. (n.d.). Retrieved September 23, 2015, from http://www.goodreads.com/quotes/408104-the-problem-with-patience-and-discipline-is-that-it-requires

[52] Napoleon Hill Quote. (n.d.). Retrieved September 23, 2015, from http://www.brainyquote.com/quotes/quotes/n/napoleonhi152875.html

have this darkness inside you. It affects your life, and it hinders you from getting better."

I took six months to prepare myself to forgive them. I was very disciplined and patient so that I would truly forgive them. It had to be unconditional forgiveness; I had not to expect anything in return, not even an apology. I just had to say: "I forgive you. I love you. I want to have a relationship with you." We hadn't had a relationship for most of our life. I was patient because it took a long time to get myself mentally, and spiritually, and emotionally where I needed to be to do that.

Then one day, I was finally able to go to them separately during the same day and have this conversation with them. They didn't know what I wanted to tell them, and it was an unbelievable experience with both of them.

That day, my healing began because I was able to forgive, and I could exercise patience in preparing myself to forgive. All of a sudden, things started to move, and just shy of two years, I was better; I had beaten my mental health challenges.

We need to get rid of the toxic things that are inside us. It takes time, patience, and persistence to get rid of those things. Stop now and think about the toxic things you need to remove from inside you.

The Trees That Grow Slower Bear the Greatest Fruit

Anybody who has an orchard will tell you that the trees that take a longer time to grow bear the greatest fruit. It is the same way with people. One of the challenges with patience is we need to do it without complaining. We need to be positive. One of the best definitions of patience that I have is "waiting without complaining." Sometimes we have to wait a long time even though we don't want to be patient. We want it now. That is not patience.

The word patience itself comes from the Latin word pati, which means to suffer, endure, or bear. Patience is the ability to tolerate the frustration, waiting, and delay without becoming agitated and upset. It's the ability to control our emotions when we're faced with difficulties. I know that we are faced with difficulties every day. Sometimes getting through the day is a major difficulty.

The challenges that we have with being patient are two-fold. First we need to be patient with the timing of God or the Universe. Second, we need to be patient with people around us. I don't know which one is more difficult. Both can be tremendous challenges.

There are two things that define you as a person. The first thing is your patience when you have nothing. Perhaps some of you are feeling like you have nothing emotionally right now. Perhaps you have no self-confidence and self-esteem. Maybe you have no hope or faith. Or maybe you have no friends. I know I have felt that way. I have said to my wife several times, "When people know the challenges that I have, sometimes I feel like a leper. When I walk around, everybody just turns and goes the other way because they don't know what to say, or they don't know what to do. They don't know how to deal with someone with mental illness."

The other thing that defines you is your attitude when you have everything. When your miracle and happiness comes, and when the fear and darkness fades away, and you start to live your life, you need to be grateful. You need to thank God and the Universe for the miracle in your life. You need to share that miracle with others and help them find theirs. That is how we keep a humble attitude.

Sometimes when we suffer deeply like I know you are, we have what is called selfish suffering. We develop a self-centered attitude, and we might throw pity parties for ourselves. All we can think about is ourselves. There is no room for anybody else. We need to realize that we are not the only ones in the world who suffer and there are others who suffer more than us.

I sometimes felt that nobody suffered as much as I did and that nobody could endure the pain that I was enduring. We need to recognize that other people are going through heartache, suffering, and pain as well. Millions of people suffer from the same things as us. When we become aware of that, we will have more compassion for others. That is the service that we talked about in a previous chapter. It helps us to reach out to those who are in pain. If we can help enough other people get what they want, we will get what we want.

I remember feeling like nobody else suffers. I believe God notices us and watches over us. It's usually through another person that He meets our needs. We're blessed by people who come into our lives. It could be for one therapy session, a five-minute conversation, a smile, or a hug. Or it could be a new friend. God puts those people into our lives to help us get better. I have had a countless number of those people.

Another reason that patience is such a challenge is that none of us struggle with precisely the same challenges, trials, or tragedies. Everybody is different. Our strengths and our weaknesses aren't the same as other people's either. Everybody has their thing that they struggle with. It might not be mental illness, but everybody has their struggles. We need to be aware of that.

Sometimes we feel that nobody has it as hard as we do. I started to feel this way after my son died. I would have pity parties, and I would feel like nobody suffered like I did. I was very angry with everyone and everything.

My coach, Kim, had a friend who she said it was important that I should meet. His name was Chris. She made arrangements for us to have lunch together.

I knew a little bit of Chris' story ahead of time. He and his family had been out driving in their car one night to get ice cream when a 17-year-old drunk driver hit them. In that accident, Chris lost his wife and three of his four children. He saw his wife take her last breath.

When we went to lunch, Chris shared with me how he had dealt with the tragic event, and how he had grown from it. As I sat across the table from him, feeling sorry for the tragedies and trials in my life, and that I had lost one child, I couldn't even comprehend losing three children and my wife all in an instant.

During our conversation, we talked about God's perfect timing. We talked about how we both believed that it was the will of God and the Universe that those members of our families were taken. Neither one of us thought it was a mistake. We believed it was supposed to happen, and our understanding was that we would see them and be with them again. We both believed that God does not make mistakes.

We talked about how it's okay to be angry with God and the Universe for what had happened. We talked about being patient and understanding that someday we would know why it happened.

Chris taught me about moving on. When we met, it had been seven years since the accident. He had remarried, and he had a couple of children with his new wife. Even though it hurt, and he had this hole in his heart, he had moved on with his life because that was what his wife and kids would have wanted him to do. They wouldn't have wanted him to curl up into a ball and wish he were dead like some of us feel when we deal with depression.

He talked about a depressed time. He talked about dealing with his emotions and trying to re-find himself and find a new normal. That is what you have to do when you lose someone; you have to find a new normal because things will never get back to how they were.

Chris taught me a lot about forgiveness, patience, timing, and blessings that come into our lives. What happened to both of us was tragic, but if I had to pick losing one child or losing three and my wife, I know which one I would pick.

He was brought into my life for a two-hour lunch. It changed my life and saved me. He is an amazing example to me. He has dedicated his life to go around speaking about how to deal with trials and tragedies in life and how to move forward. His life has turned into helping as many people as he can. I have been inspired by him to do the same thing. That is where part of this book is coming from. He is getting better through his service to others.

As I'm closing this chapter, I want to tell you about one of the most patient people in my life: my wife, Cindy. She has stood by me for almost 31 years of marriage. She has been through times of a living hell with a husband who was immensely paranoid and anxious, and full of self-doubt – not the man that she married. However, she never gave up. She stuck by me. She worked with my kids to understand and support me. She has always been my cheerleader. Maybe not all of us have that, but God will put those people in your life that you need. She is the love of my life. She is my rock.

Giving up on me was never an option for her though I always gave her that option. I said many times: "If you want to take the kids and leave, please do. I won't hold a grudge. I know it's hard." She was even asked by other people, "Why do you stay with him?" Her answer was: "If I just gave up on him and left, what kind of person does that make me?"

Now I get the chance to repay some of the time that she had to deal with a not very nice person as a husband. It has been amazing. We have fallen in love all over again – a different and new kind of love. And we have a great outlook on the future of our lives together.

American businessman and humorist Arnold H. Glasgow said: "The key to everything is patience. You get the chicken by hatching the egg, not by smashing it."[53]

---

53 Arnold H. Glasow Quote. (n.d.). Retrieved September 23, 2015, from http://www.brainyquote.com/quotes/quotes/a/arnoldhgl125821.html

Chapter 9
Key 7: Your Miracle

"There are only two ways to live your life. One is as though nothing is a miracle. The other is as though everything is a miracle."[54]
– Albert Einstein

The other chapters have built the foundation for a miracle to happen in your life by helping you shatter the chains that have held you down. Now we will talk about that miracle, which is the seventh key.

I am completely sure that miracles happen. They didn't just happen in biblical times. They don't just happen on the other side of the world. They happen all around us. There have been polls taken where people have been asked if they believe in miracles. From these polls, they have found that about 80% of people in the United States believe in miracles. One survey suggested that 73% of physicians in the U.S. believes in miracles and that 55% of those doctors say they have personally witnessed cases and results they consider to be miraculous.[55]

Miracles amaze us. They astonish us. We don't know what to make of a miracle. The word "dynamous" means "power." It also comes from the word "dynamite," and dynamite is explosive. It gets everybody's

---

[54] A Quote by Albert Einstein. (n.d.). Retrieved September 23, 2015, from http://www.goodreads.com/quotes/987-there-are-only-two-ways-to-live-your-life-one

[55] Sage. (2012, February 19). *Miracles in the Bible and Today*. Retrieved September 23, 2015, from http://commandtheraven.com/miracles-in-the-bible-and-today/

attention. It is amazing. That's what miracles are. Take a minute and think about a miracle happening in your life.

We don't just randomly go through life without purpose. The challenges, trials, and tragedies that we encounter are all parts of our journey through life, and they are there for a purpose. They are there to help us learn and grow and to turn us into who God and the Universe want us to be.

I have found that it's possible to experience a dramatic healing because it happened to me. And the keys that we have talked about so far are what helped me to get to that point. I don't know when your miracle is going to happen. I don't know what it's going to be. Mine took 40 years. I hope yours doesn't take as long. I hope that with the knowledge that I have shared in this book, you can speed up the process.

However, miracles don't happen in our timing. They happen in God and the Universe's timing. The Universe and God's timing is perfect. There were a lot of things that had to happen in my life to put me in the position to receive the miraculous change that I did. The miracle is based on your efforts, faith, and trust in life.

You need to expect a miracle to happen in your life. You need to be very clear to God and the Universe about what you want – the miracle that you desire. As I have said in almost every chapter, you need to let go of fear. If you fear that something negative and hurtful will happen, you are exercising faith, just in a negative way. You need to visualize and see yourself as how you want to be. You need to be able to close our eyes and see that the miracle has taken place. If you desire to be released from your chains of anxiety, bipolar disorder, paranoia, or an unfulfilled life, you need to see yourself that way already. You need to see yourself happy. You need to see freedom. You need to see peace. You need to see joy. You need to see the real you.

The next thing that was very significant for me was to pray. I don't know if that is significant for you. If you are open to praying, you need to pray often because prayer works. Whether you are talking to the Universe, a Higher Power or God, you need to pray for your miracle to happen. When you have prayed, you need to give it to God and the Universe and let go.

Continue to do everything you can on your end to make it happen. Jon Bon Jovi, the musician, said: "Miracles happen everyday, change your perception of what a miracle is and you'll see them all around you."[56] Miracles do happen every day. I have seen them happen in people's lives. Things happen without any explanation of why or how. They just happen.

It is when you can give more energy to your dreams than to your fears that miracles happen. When you fight to move from darkness to light, and when you are persistent, patient, serve others, and when you implement the Seven Essential Keys that we have talked about, that is when things start to happen.

My Miracles

I have experienced miracles in my life. Now I will share two that there is no explanation for. They just happened to me.

The first one happened about 15 years ago. I went to the doctor because I was exhausted. Just climbing the stairs made me bend over to try catching my breath. I had zero energy. When I was at the doctor, they did x-rays and ran several tests. The doctor's assistant put me on a treadmill and asked me to walk on it. "When do I stop?" I asked. The assistant jokingly replied: "You know when people die, they say they see a bright light? Stop when you start to see the bright light." He pushed me extremely hard.

Afterward, I sat down with the doctor who was one of the best. He said: "If tomorrow were not Thanksgiving, I would have surgery

---

[56] Jon Bon Jovi Quote. (n.d.). Retrieved September 23, 2015, from http://www.brainyquote.com/quotes/quotes/j/jonbonjovi381530.html

for you tomorrow. We're going to do it the day after Thanksgiving. If you have to go more than 500 feet, then drive. Don't walk or you could die. We need to put one or maybe two stents in the valves to your heart because there is a major blockage in your heart." He said it was very serious, and he went ahead and scheduled the surgery for the day after Thanksgiving.

The next day, on Thanksgiving, we had a lot of family at our house. We told them about my situation, and we asked them to pray. We also asked friends, church members, and our extended family to pray. I remember praying with the leader of our church in our area and receiving a blessing from him. He blessed me that a miracle would happen and that I would be fine.

The next day, I went in for the surgery, which was supposed to take several hours. In the middle of the surgery, the doctor brought me out of the anesthesia. I thought I was dreaming. He wanted to show me on the screen that the blockage in my heart was gone. He didn't want to end the surgery and have me sue him because he didn't do what he had said he was going to do. He said: "You don't need the stents. I don't know why." He said the blockage was gone. That was a miracle because there was no explanation for it.

Hugh Elliott the blogger said:

Miracles. You do not have to look for them. They are there, 24 7, beaming like radio waves all around you. Put up the antenna, turn up the volume. [...] [E]very person you talk to is a chance to change the world.[57]

Everybody you meet could be that person that the Universe or God has sent into your life to be that miracle for you or to help you get that miracle.

---

[57] Quote from Hugh Elliott. (n.d.). Retrieved September 23, 2015, from http://www.quotationspage.com/quote/32260.html

One of the most important things we have talked about is not to quit before your miracle happens. There were many times I wanted to quit, many times I wanted to give up, and many times I was sick and tired of being sick and tired. I remember being behind a big blue door in the psychiatric clinic in a hospital in Phoenix, Arizona. There I made a commitment to God and myself that I was going to get better. I was going to do everything I could and everything I was told to get better. That hope pulled me through. All I had left was hope.

Author Samuel Smiles said: "Hope… is the companion of power, and the mother of success; for who so hopes has within him the gift of miracles."[58] If you have hope strongly within you, you can receive the gift of a miracle. We have to do everything that is in our power and then let the Universe and God do the rest. They will make up for what we can't do. We have to do everything until we are mentally, physically, spiritually, and emotionally exhausted. When you feel like you just can't take anymore, that is when the Universe and God step in.

Author and speaker Jim Rohn said:

I have found in life that if you want a miracle you first need to do whatever it is you can do — if that's to plant, then plant; if it is to read, then read; if it is to change, then change; if it is to study, then study; if it is to work, then work; whatever you have to do. And then you will be well on your way of doing the labor that works miracles.[59]

It is crucial that we open our minds to all possibilities of where our miracle can come from. Miracles happen in a very natural manner, but they often come through unexpected channels. What we can't do is hold on tightly to exactly what we want the miracle to be and how we want it to happen. If you do, you might destroy the whole possibility.

---

[58] Samuel Smiles quote. (n.d.). Retrieved September 23, 2015, from http://www.brainyquote.com/quotes/quotes/s/samuelsmil126306.html

[59] *67 Jim Rohn Quotes.* (2013, February 12). Retrieved September 23, 2015, from http://www.verybestquotes.com/67-jim-rohn-quotes/

What you want is up to you. How it's going to happen is up to God and the Universe.

The reverend Robert H. Schuller said, "Impossible situations can become possible miracles."[60] I want to tell you about my miracle in the impossible situation I was in. In an earlier chapter, I mentioned that I went to my last therapist just once. I went to her when one of my friends begged me to seek help. I was about as bad as I had ever been. I was out of energy and everything else. All I had left was a little bit of hope.

So I went to see the therapist, and we began by talking about the same things that I had talked about with all the others. I told her my story; I was pretty good at it by now. Her response, however, was different from the other therapists. She said: "I feel that I can't let you leave my office today. You are so ill right now that I know that if you leave, you will take your life within an hour. So I'm not going to let you leave until we figure this out. We have to think far outside the box. We have to find something that you haven't tried." And I had tried just about everything. She continued, "We must think past medication." I had been on 45 on them. We must think past therapy. I had been to 17 therapists. "We need to get you away from being suicidal." I had made four attempts at taking my life. She came up with some wild ideas, and I thought, "This is ridiculous."

Then she paused, and she went: "I have one patient who has tried Electroconvulsive Therapy, ECT. The shorter term for it is shock treatment." I didn't know that they still did that, and I said that to her. The only picture I had in my head was Frankenstein with two electrodes stuck to his brain and electricity being sent through his head. She said: "No, they still do it. They do it at the University of Utah. I don't know if that is the solution, but we need to try something desperate."

She gave me the number to the people who managed the program, and I gave them a call. I got to speak to the most amazing woman – one

---

[60] Robert H. Schuller Quote. (n.d.). Retrieved September 23, 2015, from http://www.azquotes.com/quote/518248

of those angels we talked about earlier. She spent an hour and a half with me on the phone, trying everything she could to get me to come in because I didn't want to. I didn't have the energy for one more thing that wasn't going to work. She told me: "We have an 85% success rate of some improvement. At least come in, sit down with the doctor who runs the program, and talk to him."

Reluctantly, I went with my wife to the doctor. The doctor went through a list of medications, asking me if I had tried them. For every single name he listed, I said, "Yep, I have tried that one." That is when we got to the number 45. We talked about therapy, and we talked about everything because ECT is considered the "Last Resort" that you try after you have tried everything else. After having gone through everything, he determined that I was a candidate for ECT.

When my last name came up during our conversation, I was reminded that my father had received the same treatment decades earlier. He had been depressed to the point that he wouldn't talk. Then he had received ECT from this same doctor. At the time when my father was ill, I was so sick that my Mother did not tell me about his treatments. I didn't know anything about it until after he was better. After two treatments, it clicked for my dad, and he went back to his old self, full of energy and hope. The doctor said: "Since it worked for your dad, you should be a very good candidate." I finally decided to go through with it.

When you receive Electroconvulsive Therapy, you are in a room with a doctor, a nurse, and an anesthesiologist. First, they give you medicine. I remember the medicine burning like crazy when it went into my body to paralyze me. It paralyzes your entire body except for your hand, which they have a tourniquet on. That is how the doctor can feel the seizure. The reason they paralyze you is that if they don't, the electricity will cause you to come off the bed about 3 feet. Next, they put you out so that you don't feel anything. Then they use electricity to give you a severe seizure to jumpstart your brain.

One of my best friends Bryan took me to my first treatment. Bryan is the person I told you committed to help me whenever and however he could. I was scheduled to have 12 treatments, but I ended up having 13. My friend didn't tell me this till after all the treatments, but during my first treatment, I started to choke. Because I was paralyzed, I could not swallow. He said: "You turned different colors. You were gasping for air, and you couldn't breathe. Very quickly, they had to bring you off the medication. I thought you were going to die." He was convinced that this was my miracle. He didn't tell me that it happened until I was done with the treatments because I wouldn't have gone back. They had given me too much medicine but in the rest of the treatments, they got the amount of medicine right, and I was fine.

I was excited because my dad had two treatments, and he was better. By my sixth treatment, nothing had happened. My hope was diminishing. And since my insurance didn't pay for the treatments, I was paying for it myself, and it cost me about a year's income.

Then came the seventh treatment, and everything clicked. I felt happy and joyful – feelings I had not felt since I was a little kid. I went through the rest of the treatments, and I became a new person.

They described what happened as rebooting a computer. They had rebooted my brain. I went through all the treatments or as I call it "My Miracle." As a result, I had some significant memory loss. They said that was one of the side effects. To this day, there are things in my past I can't remember. But now it has been three years, and during those three years, I have not been depressed one time as I was before. I have also had very little anxiety in the last three years. I have had one small panic attack in this time span whereas I used to have about 10 or more a day. I have found joy. I have found happiness. I have found peace. I have found my life. It's a miracle.

They said that I would have to come back for more treatments and maintenance treatments. I haven't had to in three years. I have been able to start my own business. I have been able to dream dreams that I never felt possible. I have been lead to my purpose in life: to be a life-coach and to reach out and help other people find their miracles. I have been lead to write this book. All those years prepared me for now.

I don't know what your miracle is. It could be ECT. I don't know. I'm not promoting it. I'm just sharing how it worked for me. It could be medication. It could be therapy. It could be a book, a tape, or a talk. It could be a lot of different things. If you don't believe in miracles, perhaps you have forgotten that you are one.

Chapter 10
Your Purpose

"The two most important days in your life are the day
you were born and the day that you find out why."[61]
– Mark Twain

Up until now, we have talked about building a foundation to get to the point where you have your miracle and find your purpose in life. One of the ways to find your purpose is to find your passion. Your passion and your purpose combined leads to happiness and success.

We have reflected on how God gives his biggest challenges to his strongest children. There are many people who have achieved a great deal while battling the same things as you and I battle. Many a president, king, musician, and famous actor deal with what we deal with. Since they have found their passion and purpose, they have achieved greatness.

We have also looked at how fear can come into our lives and make it hard to want to move forward. It's like not being able to trust and believe in yourself, the true you.

Then we discussed the challenges of moving from darkness to light and how that can be scary. There will be toxic people in our life who tell us we can't do that, so we shouldn't try. Because of that, I'm serving others, which is also a key to being successful and one

---

61   A Quote by Mark Twain. (n.d.). Retrieved September 23, 2015, from http://www.
     goodreads.com/quotes/505050-the-two-most-important-days-in-your-life-are-the

of the keys to changing and getting better from the challenges that we have. We help ourselves when we take our eyes off ourselves and help other people.

We have discussed being persistent and always moving forward even though we don't want to. Some days are very difficult. We will have days where we go to bed saying: "Tomorrow I'll try harder and do better."

Then we talked about patience and putting our trust in the Universe and God, and in the Universe and God's timing, not our timing of when we want our miracle to happen.

Lastly, we talked about your miracle. We don't know what it is, and we don't know when or how it's going to come, but if you take the steps, it will happen. I had to wait for a long time for my miracle. Hopefully, you won't have to wait as long as I did. When my miracle came, I didn't care how long it had taken because of the blessings and happiness that came as a result.

The Path to Finding Your Purpose

Many mornings, I would wake up with a feeling that there was something deeper that I could be a part of. There were those dreams I had that we talked about writing down. I had the dreams, the things I wanted to do, yet all these things held me back. Take a few minutes and think about your dreams.

Over they years, I have learned to ask myself some questions that have helped me define my passion and my purpose. These are questions you need to ask yourself. You need to focus on your emotions as you answer these questions because your emotions are going to change. Perhaps you get excited, happy, joyful, or nervous. It could be any feeling. You might discover something that might be your passion when you answer these questions. Take the time now to write down detailed answers to these questions:

- What puts a big smile on your face? Is it the people in your life? Is it hobbies that you have? Is it activities that you have been part of?

- What are your favorite things to do? A lot of the time, it's something that you used to do in the past that you have stopped doing.
- What are things that you like to do now?
- What talents do you have?
- What skills do you have?
- What gifts do you have that you can share and use that might be your passion?
- What beliefs do you have?
- What process do you have that you firmly believe in, that you connect with? Is that something that could be your passion and your purpose?
- If you had the chance to talk to a large group of people, who would those people be? What would your message to them be? What would you share with them?
- If you had an hour with a large group of people, what would you do?

The purpose is the reason for your journey. The passion is the fire that lights your way. Those two things work together. Robert Brault the author said: "Never ask, What reason do I have to be happy? Instead ask, To what purpose can I attach my happiness?"[62] To what purpose can you attach your passion, that thing that stirs your soul and burns in your heart? It's a personal thing, and only you will know what that is when you find it.

If we don't find our purpose, we start to lose direction, and we end up going through life aimlessly. Are you alive or are you just breathing? Think about that. Are you alive? Is your life alive? Is your purpose there,

---

[62] Richie, A. (2015, January 7). *4 Inspiring Quotes of Purpose*. Retrieved September 23, 2015, from http://www.reallifeperfect.com/4-inspiring-quotes-of-purpose/

or are you just breathing? Are you just waking up every day with nothing you want to accomplish?

Author and poet Walter Savage Landor said: "Men, like nails, lose their usefulness when they lose their direction and begin to bend."[63] One of the things that happen when we find our purpose and we have a passion that drives us is that we can serve others. If other people have the same interest as us, we can teach them, guide them, and help them become passionate about it. It is a glorious thing to share that with other people.

In high school, I had a photography teacher named Mr. Dobson. Before then, I had never taken pictures, so I didn't know anything about photography. I just signed up for it. Mr. Dobson was the sort of teacher who could change someone's life. The reason was that he had a passion and a purpose in teaching photography. He was a world-renowned wildlife photographer. His work had been published, and his photographs were all over the world. He retired from that just to teach kids to have a passion for photography.

My friend and I were two of his students, and Mr. Dobson took a special interest in us. On Saturdays during the summer months, he would take us to different parts of the state where we would take pictures. He taught us everything he knew. He found a passion for photography in us, and he pulled out that passion. He made such an impact on us that to this day, over 30 years later, we both still do professional photography, and that has been our love. He found his purpose, and he shared it with us. That is what we can do as we get a miracle and change. That's what I do now. My passion and my purpose have changed. I love photography, and that was a passion of mine, but that led me to my purpose, which is to help other people who deal with mental illness challenges. My purpose is to teach them what I know and help them achieve greatness in their lives.

---

[63] Walter Savage Landor Quote. (n.d.). Retrieved September 23, 2015, from http://www.brainyquote.com/quotes/quotes/w/waltersava142586.html

"The purpose of life is a life of purpose."[64] Robert Burns said that. At the moment, you are in the process, and you might be getting close to your miracle. What will happen on the way is that you will change, become more positive, and accomplish more things.

In the process, fear will jump back in. You need to slay your inner demons of fear and doubt, and you need to be careful whom you share our dreams with. Are you sharing them with people who will cheer you on? Or are you sharing them with toxic people who tell you that you can't do it?

It's almost better not to share it with very many people because they will tear you down. Stephen Covey, one of my favorite authors, said:

Now, when you define your purpose, a purpose that shakes your heart and stirs your soul, that's when conscious living begins. That's because you know now what you stand for and your place in this world. While it doesn't mean that everything suddenly becomes rosy and all your problems disappear, at least you now have clarity of what you want to drive in this world. This subsequently helps you to set long-term goals that move you in the right direction (toward your purpose).[65]

Begin by making some short-term goals. Then make action plans, and then take daily actions. Then you start to move, and you start to move faster. Your mind will work to find better and bigger things to do, and you begin to think bigger. The Universe and God will connect you with people who will help you get to where you need to go. That has happened to me time after time. Now I'm connected with people who were not part of my life before, and they are helping me achieve my dreams.

---

64   Robert Bryne Quote. (n.d.). Retrieved September 23, 2015, from
      https://www.goodreads.com/author/show/1707476.Robert_Bryne
65   Personal Excellence (n.d.). Why Have a Life Purpose? 5 Reasons You Should
      Have a Purpose. [Web log post] Retrieved September 23, 2015, from
      http://personalexcellence.co/blog/why-have-a-life-purpose

Doubt is going to jump in again. Life Coach Martha Beck said: "The 'yeah' pushes us toward our passion; the 'but' stops us dead in our tracks. Yeah-but prefaces infinite justifications for avoiding the things our hearts find compelling."[66] We need to move from darkness to light. We need to be positive. We need to let go and let the Universe and God take care of it. As you do this, ask yourself:

- How do I want to feel on the inside as I'm going through this?
- Do I want to feel truthful, reverential, scared?
- Do I want to have doubts?
- Do I want to be positive?
- Do I want to dream?
- Do I want to accomplish great things?
- Do I tell myself I can't do it, or am I constantly telling myself I can and I will, and taking those little steps toward my miracle and finding my purpose?

The reality is that if you don't decide what your life is about and find your purpose, your life becomes about how you spend your day and what you do. If you don't have a purpose and passion, how you spend the day is usually not very important. It's not taking you anywhere. You're just breathing instead of being alive. Take a few minutes and think about the choices of just breathing or really being alive.

"When he walks he casts a shadow of purpose,"[67] said Anthologist Terri Guillemets. When a confident person walks into a room, he or she cast a shadow of purpose. They know where they are going. They are confident. Do they have doubts? Yes. Do they have fears? Yes. But their

---

[66] Beck, M. (n.d.). *How to Find Your Passion*. Retrieved September 23, 2015, from http://www.oprah.com/omagazine/How-to-Find-Your-Passion-Martha-Beck

[67] QuoteMinder. (2012, October 28). "When he walks he casts a shadow of purpose." ~Terri Guillemets #quotes [Tweet] Retrieved from https://twitter.com/quoteminder

goal, their dream, and their purpose are bigger than their fears. They are going to be victorious no matter what because they will never give up. They will be patient and persistent.

Christopher Reeve, who played Superman and then had a terrible accident, leaving him in a wheelchair, said: "So many of our dreams at first seem impossible, then they seem improbable, and then, when we summon the will, they soon become inevitable."[68]

I didn't know how my dream was going to happen. I did everything I could, and then I turned it over to God and the Universe. In the last chapter, I shared with you when my dreams started to come true and when my miracle happened. At the time, I was as low as I had ever been, but I didn't give up. That was when everything happened, and my life changed quickly and drastically for the better.

My passion resonates with my purpose. Sometimes they are the same thing. The passion that I have had for over 30 years was photography. Through my depression and other mental health challenges, it was something that I enjoyed. I was good at it, and people loved my work. It allowed me to meet a lot of amazing people in the process, and I got to capture many unbelievable moments for people.

But as I said, the Universe and God bring people into our lives, sometimes miraculously, to make our life better and to be those angels that help us attain the things we want.

I do a lot of fashion photography, and I'm always contacting models to help them with their work. A little over a year ago, it was the other way around; a model contacted me. She contacted me via e-mail, and she wrote that she loved my work and would like to work with me. I talked with her a little bit, and I set up a date for a photo shoot with her a few days from then. Since she was 16 years old, I told her that she would need to bring one of her parents. She was okay with that and

---

[68] Christopher Reeve Quote. (n.d.). Retrieved September 23, 2015, from http://www.brainyquote.com/quotes/quotes/c/christophe125724.html

said that she would bring her mother. I had never talked to this person before. She lived over 40 miles away from me. There was no way she and I would have met her if she hadn't called me.

Since I used to have so much fear in my life for several years, I would always look on the Internet for a good book on fear. The night before the mother and daughter came to my studio for the photoshoot, I found a book on Amazon that I downloaded. I stayed up most of the night reading it, and it was exactly what I was looking for because it provided a lot of guidance and help. As I was just about to finish reading it, I left it open on my computer in my studio.

The next day, the young model came to my studio with her mother. While she was getting ready for the photoshoot, I talked to her mother, asking her what she did for a living. She told me she was a life coach and that she had just published a book.

"What's the name of your book?" I asked out of curiosity.

"It's called *The Path to Fearlessness*," she said.

In amazement, I told her "I read your book last night."

Then I showed her the computer screen. We both went silent. Immediately, we realized that this was a lot more than a photo shoot. We understood that we had been brought together for a purpose. She was there to help me fill in the missing pieces of my recovery and change. God and the Universe already knew that my son was going to die eight months later, and she was my angel that came into my life at the perfect time.

It was an instant bond and friendship, the kind that usually takes years to develop. Some people would call our meeting a coincidence. I don't. I call that a miracle. Out of the millions of books that are available, I bought hers. Out of all the millions of people where I live, she was in my studio.

We talked further and had a beautiful shoot with her daughter. Then I said:

"I probably can't afford life coaching. It's probably very expensive."

"Well, I'm sure that my daughter's portfolio that you're going to do for her is not cheap either," she replied.

So we agreed to trade. I would do the portfolio for free, and she would do the coaching for free.

I started coaching with her. That was the final piece of the puzzle to my recovery. I told you I had the shock treatment and that I was trying to find out what happiness was because I hadn't been happy in over 40 years. I didn't know how to act. I didn't know how to think. I didn't know how to make decisions because I had been depressed for so long.

The coaching filled all those voids and made me complete. During about three-quarters of the way through her training, she told me that she strongly felt that I needed to be a coach and share my story with others. She believed that there were thousands of people out there I could help, and she thought that was why I had gone through everything I had.

I thought about it and prayed about it because that is what I do. Then I got the same answer. So I went through more training with her and became a certified coach because that was my purpose. I had gone through everything I was supposed to go through in my life for 40 years to get to the point where I could help other people.

My passion all those years was photography and I loved it, but it wasn't my purpose. My purpose was to be a life coach and help other people who have the same struggles as I have and give them hope, a path, and these keys that could help them have a fulfilled life and live the rest of their lives happy.

When you get that clarity, that doesn't mean your life's going to be perfect. For six weeks after I became certified, I was as happy as I have ever been in my entire life. My thoughts were clear, I knew what I was doing, and I was making good decisions. I was getting ready to serve people for the rest of my life. I could honestly say my life couldn't be any better.

Six weeks later, my son died. The Universe and God in their perfect timing put me in a position where I could handle it when that happened. I didn't go backward. I didn't get depressed. I didn't get full of stress and panic. I had been prepared for that experience to happen.

Then my story got even bigger. Now I can speak to a whole new group of people that have lost children because I know what it feels like.

I will end this book with one of my favorite quotes that I found years ago. I share it along with my dreams, hopes, and prayers for you. Your miracle can come true, and you can prepare yourself for it by using the Seven Essential Keys.

Early in the book, I said you can't just read about them. You have to follow them. You have to build your support system. You have to get rid of the toxic people in your life. You have to find those friends that you can trust, and the right doctors, therapists, psychiatrists, and psychologists and the medication. I don't know where your miracle is going to come from, but you have to build that structure around you. Then you have to go to work and fight for your life.

Here is my wish for you, as journalist and author Hunter S. Thompson said it:

Life should not be a journey to the grave with the intention of arriving safely in a pretty and well preserved body, but rather to skid in [the grave] broadside in a cloud of smoke, thoroughly used up, totally worn out, and loudly proclaiming "Wow! What a Ride![69]

I pray that you have that ride.

---

[69] A Quote from The Proud Highway. (n.d.). Retrieved September 23, 2015, from http://www.goodreads.com/quotes/47188-life-should-not-be-a-journey-to-the-grave-with

Contact the Author

Life Coaching by Greg Thredgold
(801) 400-6124
claritycoachgreg@gmail.com

Made in the USA
Las Vegas, NV
06 January 2021

15444716R00056